Effective
Presentation

Effective Presentation

Sarah Dickinson

ORION
BUSINESS
BOOKS

The right of Sarah Dickinson to identified as the
author of this work has been asserted by her in accordance with the
Copyright, Designs and Patents Act 1988

First published in Great Britain in 1998 by
Orion Business
An imprint of The Orion Publishing Group Ltd
Orion House, 5 Upper St Martin's Lane, London WC2H 9EA

A CIP catalogue record for this book
is available from the British Library

ISBN 0–75281–214–9

Typeset by Deltatype, Birkenhead, Merseyside
Printed in Great Britain by
Clays Ltd, St Ives plc.

Contents

To Jo and the people of Montserrat

Acknowledgements
I am very grateful for the help, encouragement and support from Kay Avila, Val Bethell, Jilly Carter, 'Dickie' Dickinson, Brenda Ellison, Annie Garthwaite, Alli Godbold, Susan Henry, Andrew Hewson, Jim Hiley, John Hitchens, John Renton, Clive Roslin and Iona Salinger whose editing has been invaluable.

Introduction

Why is it that man can land space buggies on Mars and design microchips smaller than pin heads but still have difficulty in coming up with a winning formula for overcoming a fear of speaking in public, especially in a business environment?

Nearly everyone will cite giving presentations as one of the most daunting aspects of their work. No one likes having to give them, and few believe that they are any good at doing so. The reason for this lack of confidence is usually fear of failing in public, an anxiety that often becomes a self-fulfilling prophecy. The speaker is convinced that he or she is no good at talking in front of an audience and proves it by giving a lacklustre performance.

Because presentations are nowadays such an integral part of any business person's life, ways have to be found to overcome this fear to such an extent that every presentation can be viewed not just as a business opportunity but as a career opportunity as well. This book is written for anyone in business who has to speak in front of an audience, whether graduate trainee, middle manager or chief executive. It will show her how to overcome fear, the skills needed to write and give a presentation, and how to set about perfecting them to the point that speaking becomes a pleasure rather than a dread.

It is comforting to recognise that there is no such thing as a natural orator. Natural performer, yes; natural orator, no. Winston Churchill's rallying 'we'll fight them on the beaches' speech appeared to be a spontaneous outburst of patriotic fervour. More likely it evolved from his own 'blood, sweat and tears' of meticulous preparation. That discipline, combined with a bulldog voice and a consummate sense of timing and theatre, created one of the twentieth century's finest speakers.

Sadly, perhaps because of our natural reticence or apathy, there are few orators today who can match his skills. Yet, because of the proliferation of communication outlets and high expectations, ever greater demands are made on us all to perform to a high standard. No longer is it acceptable to shuffle on to a stage, read haltingly from a script and think 'that'll do' – it won't.

This book won't transform the shy, stuttering spokesperson into a galvanizing performer overnight, but it will equip such a speaker with the skills to prepare and present a speech in a variety of situations, and to deal confidently with questions from an audience. It will also show how to:

- plan, write and time a speech
- dress appropriately
- command audience attention
- overcome anxiety
- improve voice quality
- deal with nervous physical mannerisms
- vary pitch and pace
- cope with fluffs and blunders
- introduce humour
- use visual aids, microphones, notes and an autocue
- answer questions
- deal with unexpected interruptions
- be interviewed
- hold a press conference or press briefing.

Speaking in front of an audience is an opportunity not a sentence. What a pity to miss that opportunity because of fear or lack of confidence. How much better to recognise the value in self-esteem and business success if you master how to do it.

Chapter 1
The art of public speaking

'To conquer fear is the beginning of wisdom.'

(Bertrand Russell, *An Outline of Intellectual Rubbish*)

For many years I've had a recurring nightmare that, until I talked about it, I was convinced was unique. Setting aside what might lie behind my elevated theatrical status in the dream, I still consider that the experience bears all the hallmarks of the typical nocturnal brain games that trick us momentarily into believing that our professional or emotional end is nigh.

The scene is always the same. It's about twenty minutes after curtain-up at the National Theatre. It's the first night of a new production of Macbeth, in which I have my first major role. I stand in the wings. Duncan is speaking.

> True, worthy Banquo: he is full so valiant;
> And in his commendations I am fed;
> It is a banquet to me. Let's after him,
> Whose care is gone before to bid us welcome.
> It is a peerless kinsman.
>
> [*Macbeth*, Act One, Scene V]

It's the turn of Lady Macbeth. My first chance to make contact with the audience. I'm in Inverness, in Macbeth's castle and I have a letter in my hand ... The words should come easily:

> They met me in the day of success; and I have learn'd by ...

Nothing happens. The letter and mind is blank. I can't remember a single word. At that moment, when public humiliation seems inevitable, I always wake in a state of palpitating anxiety before realising that the experience was only a dream.

It doesn't require a degree in psychology to analyse the cause of my unconscious distress, nor would I be surprised if its theatrical setting isn't one shared by many. As the dream invariably occurs prior to participation in a broadcast or delivery of a presentation, I am presumably living out my anxiety as to whether or not I am insufficiently prepared for the forthcoming task. I have had to learn to heed these nocturnal warnings and also, however rigorously I have prepared, to conquer the basic fear of performing in front of an audience. You must too, so that you can take advantage of the personal or company gains that public performance potentially offers. Remember that a basic lack of confidence – what celebrated novelist Fay Weldon refers to as a fear of being 'found out' – is a common trait and it *can be overcome*.

It will help you to tackle the challenge of giving a presentation if you accept that this is not a natural thing to do. Standing alone in front of a group of people, in anthropological terms, isn't sensible. You are completely outnumbered, usually unarmed, and almost invariably your back is to the wall. You might have the slender advantage of speaking from a raised platform, but that bonus is quickly expunged by the knowledge that, for however long you've been billed to speak, there is no retreat – unless, of course, things get really too hot to handle and you opt for the dire last resort (which a colleague promises me he once did) of feigning a heart attack, a ploy best used sparingly!

Not surprisingly, over the years spokespeople have evolved a few subtle weapons and some protective barriers. The solid opaque lectern serves as a useful defensive tool because it prevents sight of trembling knees and tap-dancing feet, gives the presenter's body much needed physical support, and provides a home for mental ammunition in the form of notes. The overhead or slide projector has also been developed to serve as a tactical diversion. The value of the visual aid used to lie in its ability to clarify or enhance the speaker's text; unfortunately, it is used far too often these days as a crutch for the speaker rather than as a useful communication tool.

When it comes to dress, the jury is still out as to whether an artful choice of wardrobe can help a speaker feel less vulnerable. If, like Screaming Lord Sutch, a much-missed candidate in the UK's

1997 general election, you dress flamboyantly, you might feel secure behind the costume and your audience might enjoy your performance, but they may not remember a word of its content. If, on the other hand, you deliberately dress to be unremarkable, you risk failing to seize your audience's attention from the outset.

One of the secrets to delivering a perfect presentation is to be confident enough to be able to do so with as few props as possible. Very few people, however, have the confidence or experience to speak without any notes or visual aids. One of the aims of this book is to help reduce your presentational dependencies to an absolute minimum, so liberating you to *perform*, rather than simply *present*.

➡ **FOUR EXAMPLES**

There are many things you need to do before you reach the cosmetic decisions of what to wear and what kind of visual aids to use. The two vital elements of a successful presentation, apart from an ability to perform, are your audience and your text. To illustrate how inextricable they are, I have chosen four extracts from speeches given by international figures. Nelson Mandela, Adolf Hitler, Neil Kinnock and Ronald Reagan. Even though style and structure differ, all four demonstrate a keen awareness of their audience and their ability to write clearly.

Nelson Mandela

Nelson Mandela is not blessed with great oratorical skills. He is quietly spoken and not given to flamboyant gestures. It is therefore the content of his speeches on which he has to rely for impact. In this respect, he is a master.

What follows is an edited extract from the closing moments of his four-hour defence to the Johannesburg court on 20 April 1964, having been charged under South Africa's Suppression of Communism Act and facing the death penalty. His immediate audience was the Court, but he knew that in reality he would be talking to the world. The strength of these closing passages lies in their logical structure, Mandela's use of repetition and a courageous climax.

Our fight is against real, and not imaginary hardships or, to use the language of the State Prosecutor, 'so-called hardships'. We fight against two features which are the hallmarks of African life in South Africa, and which are entrenched by legislation which we seek to have repealed. These features are poverty and lack of human dignity, and we do not need Communists, or so-called 'agitators' to teach us about these things. The whites enjoy what may well be the highest standard of living in the world, whilst Africans live in poverty and misery ...

The complaint of Africans, however, is not only that they are poor and whites are rich, but that the laws which are made by the whites are designed to preserve this situation.

There are two ways to break out of poverty. The first is by formal education, and the second is by the worker acquiring a greater skill at this work and thus higher wages. As far as Africans are concerned, both these avenues of advancement are deliberately curtailed by legislation. The present Government has always sought to hamper Africans in their search for education. There is compulsory education for all white children at virtually no cost to their parents, be they rich or poor. Similar facilities are not provided for African children. ... The present Prime Minister said during the debate on the Bantu Education Bill in 1953: 'When I have control of Native education, I will reform it so that Natives will be taught from childhood to realise that equality with Europeans is not for them. ... People who believe in equality are not desirable teachers for Natives. ...'

The other main obstacle to the economic advancement of the Africans is the industrial colour bar by which all better jobs of industry are reserved for whites only. Moreover, Africans are not allowed to form trade unions, which have recognition under the Industrial Conciliation Act. The Government often answers its critics by saying that Africans in South Africa are economically better off than the inhabitants of the other countries in Africa. Our complaint is not that we are poor by comparison with people in other countries, but that we are poor by comparison with white people in our own country, and that we are prevented by legislation from altering this imbalance.

Hundreds and thousands of Africans are thrown into gaol each year under pass laws. Even worse than this is the fact that pass laws keep husband and wife apart and lead to the breakdown of family life. Poverty and the breakdown of family life have secondary effects. Children wander about the streets of the townships because they have no schools to go to, or no money to enable them to go to school, or no parents at home to see that they go to school because both parents, if there be two, have to work to keep the family alive. This leads to a breakdown in moral standards, to an alarming rise in illegitimacy and to growing violence which erupts, not only politically but everywhere. ... People are afraid to walk alone in the streets after dark. Housebreakings and robberies are increasing despite the fact that the death sentence can now be imposed for such offences. Death sentences cannot cure the festering sore. The only cure is to alter the conditions under which the Africans are forced to live, and to meet their legitimate grievances.

We want to be part of the general population, and not confined to living in our ghettos. African men want to have their wives and children to live with them where they work, and not to be forced into an unnatural existence in men's hostels. Our women want to be left with their men folk, and not to be left permanently widowed in the Reserves. We want to be allowed out after 11 p.m. and not to be confined to our rooms like little children. We want to be allowed to travel in our own country, and seek work where we want to, and not where the Labour Bureau tells us to. We want a just share in the whole of South Africa; we want security and a stake in society.

Above all, my lord, we want equal political rights, because without them our disabilities will be permanent. I know this sounds revolutionary to the whites in this country, because the majority of voters will be Africans. This makes the white man fear democracy. But this fear cannot be allowed to stand in the way of the only solution which will guarantee racial harmony and freedom for all. It is not true that the enfranchisement of all will result in racial domination. Political division, based on colour, is entirely artificial, and when it disappears, so will the domination of one colour group by another. The ANC has spent half a century fighting against racialism. When it triumphs, as it certainly must, it will not change that policy.

This, then, is what the ANC is fighting. Our struggle is a truly national one. It is a struggle of the African people, inspired by our own suffering and our own experience. It is a struggle for the right to live. During my lifetime I have dedicated my life to this struggle of the African people. I have fought against white domination, and I have fought against black domination. I have cherished the ideal of a democratic and free society in which all persons live together in harmony with equal opportunities. It is an ideal which I hope to live for, and to see realised. But my lord, if needs be, it is an ideal for which I am prepared to die.

We can test the structure of this extract by paraphrasing the text in two different ways. If we were to simply write a précis of the speech, it might look like this:

Africans seek the repeal of laws that deprive them of human dignity and condemn them to poverty. The poverty trap can be ended through education, and human dignity restored by repeal of the pass laws. However, the South African Government [of the time] shows no sign of wishing to do either. The secondary effects of this reluctance to change the status of Africans will result in further social decay and increased violence. Africans want many things and will maintain the struggle to achieve them. Nelson Mandela is prepared to die for his ideals.

If the speech was condensed to its main points on cue cards, it might look as shown in Figure 1.1.

Despite the relentless logic of his arguments, Nelson Mandela failed to persuade his detractors and he was sentenced to life imprisonment. He wasn't able to speak in public again for 26 years, but when he did he talked to a crowd of fifty thousand and a television audience of millions.

Logic and structure, of course, is only one side of the oratorical coin. The difference between a brilliant and an average speech often lies in the delivery. However artfully crafted, if a speech is delivered in a monotone, the impact of the message can be lost. Ironically, the reverse is not always true: it is possible, however

CURRENT LEGISLATION results in
loss of HUMAN DIGNITY
continued POVERTY
(examples)

1

RESOLUTION through
EDUCATION
IMPROVED WORK SKILLS

2

FRUSTRATION by
NO GOVT. COMMITMENT
INDUSTRIAL COLOUR BAR
ILLEGAL TRADE UNIONS

3

SECONDARY effects of POVERTY
and BREAKDOWN OF FAMILY LIFE
REDUCED MORAL STANDARDS
ILLEGITIMACY
VIOLENCE

4

DEMANDS
Integration
Reunited families
No curfew
Freedom to travel
Security and status in society
Equal political rights

5

COMMITMENT
Struggle
Sacrifice

6

Figure 1.1: Nelson Mandela's speech summarised on cue cards.

doubtful the message, to deliver a speech with such energy and commitment that an audience will be persuaded, whatever the content.

Adolf Hitler

Adolf Hitler still stands as the prime exponent of this art, and his skill can be seen in an extract from the closing passages of a two-hour speech he made before the Reichstag on 13 July 1934, in which he achieved his ambition of establishing a one-party system in Germany.

If anyone reproaches me and asks why I did not resort to the regular courts of justice for conviction of the offenders, then all that I can say to him is this: in this hour I was responsible for the fate of the German people, and thereby I became the supreme justiciary of the German people! ...

When in March of last year our young revolution stormed through Germany, my highest endeavour was to shed as little blood as possible. To millions of my former opponents, on behalf of the new state and in the name of the National Socialist Party, I offered a general amnesty; millions of them have since joined us and are loyally co-operating in the rebuilding of the Reich.

I hoped that it might not be necessary any longer to be forced to defend this state yet again with arms in our hands. But since fate has now nonetheless put us to this test, all of us wish to pledge ourselves with only the greater fanaticism to hold fast to that which was formerly won at the price of the blood of so many of our best men and which today had to be maintained once more through the blood of German fellow countrymen. Just as one-and-a-half years ago I offered reconciliation to our former opponents, so would I from henceforth also promise forgetfulness to all those who shared in the guilt of this act of madness. Let them bethink themselves, and remembering this melancholy calamity in our new German history let them devote themselves to the task of reparation.

May they now recognise with surer insight than before the great task that fate sets us, which civil war and chaos cannot perform. May we all feel responsible for the most precious treasure that there can be for the German people – internal order, internal and external peace – just as I am ready to undertake responsibility at the bar of history for the twenty-four hours in which the bitterest decisions of my life were made, in which fate once again taught me in the midst of anxious care with every thought to hold fast to the dearest thing that has been given us in this world: the German people and the German Reich!

So persuasive were his perorations that, within an hour of the death of President von Hindenburg and despite blatant abuse of the law and civil liberties, he was made Head of State as well as Supreme Commander of the Armed Forces of the Reich. I suspect it was passion rather than content that helped win the day.

Neil Kinnock

In the third example, we see Neil Kinnock, former leader of Britain's Labour party, combining the skills of *repetition* and *rhythm* to emphasise his argument. This memorable speech, delivered on the eve of the UK's 1993 general election, was Kinnock's last attempt to turn the electorate against the incumbent Prime Minister, Margaret Thatcher. He invoked every Welsh fibre in his body.

If Margaret Thatcher is re-elected as Prime Minister, *I warn you*.
I warn you that you will have pain –
When healing and relief depend upon payment.
I warn you that you will have ignorance –
When talents are untended and wits are wasted, when learning is a privilege and not a right.
I warn you that you will have poverty –
When pensions slip and benefits are whittled away by a Government that won't pay in an economy that can't pay.
I warn you that you will be cold –
When fuel charges are used as a tax system that the rich don't notice and the poor can't afford.
I warn you that you must not expect work –
When many cannot spend, more will not be able to earn. When

they don't earn, they don't spend. When they don't spend, work dies.

I warn you not to go into the streets alone after dark or into the streets in large crowds of protest in the light.

I warn you that you will be quiet –

When the curfew of fear and the gibbet of unemployment make you obedient.

I warn you that you will have defence of a sort –

With a risk and at a price that passes all understanding.

I warn you that you will be home-bound –

When fares and transport bills kill leisure and lock you up.

I warn you that you will borrow less –

When credit, loans, mortgages and easy payments are refused to people on your melting income.

If Margaret Thatcher wins, she will be more a Leader than a Prime Minister. That power produces arrogance and when it is toughened by Tebbitry and flattered and fawned upon by spineless sycophants, the boot-licking tabloid knights of Fleet Street and placemen in the quangos, the arrogance corrupts absolutely.

If Margaret Thatcher wins –

I warn you not be ordinary.

I warn you not to be young.

I warn you not to fall ill.

I warn you not to get old.

By introducing each stanza with the phrase 'I warn', Kinnock relentlessly hammers home his message of doubt and reinforces it by expressing his ideas in short, rhythmic sentences. It wasn't enough, however, to get his party re-elected.

Ronald Reagan

The final example is evidence of the effectiveness of the use of *everyday language* when trying to communicate with a very large audience. Ronald Reagan was an exemplar of someone who knew how to do this. He could reach into our hearts and make us feel as if he was talking to each one of us directly.

His television address to the nation after the catastrophic explosion of the space shuttle *Challenger* on 28 January 1986 illustrates the power of his direct, simple, moving style.

Nineteen years ago, almost to the day, we lost three astronauts in a terrible accident on the ground. But we've never lost an astronaut in flight; we've never had a tragedy like this. And perhaps we've forgotten the courage it took for the crew of the shuttle; but they, the Challenger Seven, were aware of the dangers, but overcame them and did their jobs brilliantly. We mourn seven heroes: Michael Smith, Dick Scobee, Judith Resnik, Ronald McNair, Ellison Onizuka, Gregory Jarvis and Christa McAuliffe. We mourn their loss as a nation together.

For families of the seven, we cannot bear, as you do, the full impact of this tragedy. But we feel the loss, and we're thinking about you so very much. Your loved ones were daring and brave, and they had that special grace, that special spirit that says, 'Give me a challenge and I'll meet it with joy.' They had a hunger to explore the universe and discover its truths. They wished to serve, and they did. They served all of us. We've grown used to wonders in this century. It's hard to dazzle us. But for twenty-five years, the United States' space programme has been doing just that. We've grown used to the idea of space, and perhaps we forget that we've only just begun. We're still pioneers. They, the members of the *Challenger* crew, were pioneers.

And I want to say something to the schoolchildren of America who were watching the live coverage of the shuttle's takeoff. I know it is hard to understand, but sometimes painful things like this happen. It's all part of the process of exploration and discovery. It's all part of taking a chance and expanding man's horizons. The future doesn't belong to the faint-hearted; it belongs to the brave. The *Challenger* crew was pulling us into the future, and we'll continue to follow them.

There's a coincidence today. On this day three hundred and ninety years ago, the great explorer Sir Francis Drake died aboard ship off the coast of Panama. In his lifetime the great frontiers were the oceans, and a historian later said, 'He lived by the sea, died on it, and was buried in it'. Well, today we can say of the *Challenger* crew: Their dedication was, like Drake's, complete.

The crew of the space shuttle *Challenger* honoured us by the manner in which they lived their lives. We will never forget them, nor the last time we saw them, this morning, as they prepared for the journey and waved goodbye and 'slipped the surly bonds of earth' to 'touch the face of God'.

With the help of speech-writer Peggy Noonan, Reagan touched an emotional chord in every American. He used everyday superlatives like 'daring' 'briliantly', 'dazzle' to convey a nation's pride in its heroes. He likened the *Challenger* crew to past explorers, and he even managed to turn the tragedy into a continued commitment to space exploration. Most artful of all, he closed his speech with lines from the poem 'High Flight' written by John Gillespie Magee, a Canadian pilot who flew Spitfires during the Second World War, and who was killed at the age of nineteen.

➡ WHAT NEXT?

As those brief extracts demonstrate, even though their language and styles differ and you may not agree with their ideologies, all four speakers knew precisely at whom they were aiming their thoughts and what they wanted to say. I list in Appendix A twenty 'golden rules' for effective speeches and presentations, and each is explained further in the course of this book. The following chapters will show you how to get to grips with your audience, formulate your thoughts and give your presentation with verve and energy.

Chapter 2
Where do you start?

A journey of a thousand miles must begin with a single step.

Before getting anywhere near the word processor, there is some essential preliminary research to be done. Find out as much as possible about your audience.

I recently gave two presentations on the same day as part of a seminar on weather preparedness in the Caribbean. My task was to help both audiences learn how to handle the media in the wake of a crisis – in this case, a hurricane. When I began to research the audience, it quickly became clear that, although tourism was the common interest, the message to each group needed to be subtly different.

The morning's audience came from the public sector: UK representatives of Caribbean tourist boards, whose mission was to represent a particular country and promote its tourist attractions. This audience would want to know how a country should deal nationally with the media in the event of a crisis. The afternoon was made up of operations managers of UK-based tour operators who, unlike the tourist boards, were privately funded and had customers and shareholders to answer to. Not only was their experience of the media likely to be quite extensive, but they would also want to know specifically how to tailor their messages to satisfy both customers and shareholders. Being forewarned of the make-up of each audience, I was able not only to adapt my basic presentation to the specific needs of each group but also to anticipate questions.

➡ KNOW YOUR AUDIENCE

So, what information do you need to know about your audience in order to help you decide what you're going to say? Simply:

- size
- names
- age/sex ratio/race
- status/title
- company representation

Researching this list will give you the following valuable information and enable you to determine the likely level of the competence of the group and whether there are any racial or political sensitivities. Once these basic facts are established, you will then be able to begin to assess the level of expectation.

Size

It sounds obvious, but until you know the likely size of an audience, you won't be able to start structuring your presentation. If you know that there will be a maximum of 40 people, you will be able to adopt a fairly informal approach, taking advantage of the relative intimacy of the occasion. If, on the other hand, that number swells to 400, you will need to be more disciplined and more formal. This is simply because it is harder to keep the attention of 400 than it is 40 (see Chapter 6 on performance techniques).

Names

Unless you're addressing a genuinely open public meeting that anyone, so long as they aren't deemed to be a public nuisance, can attend, it is usually possible to obtain a list of delegates and their titles prior to the event. It is important that you obtain this list as soon as you can, for it will provide the answers to key questions about your audience that, in turn, will help determine what you say.

Age/sex ratio/race

Knowing the age, sex ratio and race of the audience will help to target your speech. For example, you would know that a presentation about pensions would need to be pitched very differently to a group of undergraduates than it would to middle managers on short-term contracts. Similarly, if you are talking to a dedicated religious group about crime in our inner cities, you would know that you would have to deal with the issue of culpability very carefully.

Knowing the 'male/female' ratio is also helpful. I'm sure many women have sat through speeches where it is obvious that the speaker hasn't even considered the possibility of a female presence and proceeded to pepper his remarks with, at best, sexist comments and, at worst, smutty humour. There is much discussion about women being better listeners than men and more able to share their feelings. So long as you are well prepared and are aware of the techniques of speech-making, it shouldn't matter what sex either you or your audience is.

Status/title

Giving a speech is often a useful promotional stepping stone. If you know that your boss is going to be in the audience, you can weave a subtle mention of his presence into your text. Your preparation may also reveal the presence of someone in the audience far senior to anyone else, in which case you may need to encourage all participants to believe themselves to be of equal value. Foreknowledge may also give you the opportunity to involve one or two people directly. For instance, it may enable you to ask someone a prearranged question, or 'plant' some end-of-speech questions.

Company representation

Knowing before you begin to draft your presentation which organisations or companies will be represented in the audience is invaluable. On a purely selfish level, you may be able to use your speech to pitch subtly for a new job. More important is the fact that knowing which companies are to be there will alert you to the advisability of revealing competitively sensitive information.

➡ WHAT IS THE SUBJECT?

Now that you have a feel for what your audience will be like, you can turn your attention to the overall subject of the event.

Let's assume that you've been invited to be one of several speakers at a seminar to be attended by middle management. The subject of the seminar is the impact on business of the media explosion. Whilst it will be the organiser's job to co-ordinate all the speeches, there is nothing to stop you from putting forward ideas. If, for example, your expertise lies in the financial sector, you will make much more impact if you can relate the overall subject to your specific knowledge. *Everyone can speak more fluently and more convincingly on their specialist subject.*

➡ WHAT DOES THE AUDIENCE EXPECT?

Once you've established a general profile of your audience and the subject of the seminar or lecture, you can begin to assess their expectations. Are they there to hear something new, or will they feel more comfortable going over old ground? How much do they know already? Are they the kind of audience who will respond well to provocation? Are they expecting to be persuaded to your point of view? Will they be surprised if you ask for audience participation? Addressing these questions greatly assists when it comes to the moment of committal – putting words into the computer in order to formulate your presentation.

➡ HOUSEKEEPING

Although the information gleaned from answers to these questions will probably equip you sufficiently to start structuring your speech, there are a few sensible additional 'housekeeping' points to establish. These are given in Checklist 2.1. It is a long list and there is a lot of work to do, but it will be worth taking the trouble.

Checklist 2.1   **Initial information required about a speaking engagement**

- What type of venue and seating plan exists?
- What should you wear?
- Who will be in the chair?
- Who are the other speakers?
- In what order will the speakers participate?
- How long will your speech be?
- Will there be visual aids?
- Will there be sound or autocue facilities?
- Will there be a height-adjustable lectern?
- Will there be questions from the floor?
- Will the presentation be recorded?
- Will the media be there?
- Should you provide copies of your presentation, or other publicity material?
- Will you be expected to stay on after the presentation?
- Will the audience be charged admittance and will you charge a fee?

What type of venue and seating plan exists?

The location and size of the venue will often determine the style of your presentation. One of the first questions you should ask when you're invited to give a talk is where will the event be held? Knowing the precise location will help you plan. Will you need to take a day off work? Will you have to stay overnight? Is the venue close enough to get to a rehearsal? Will you be able to change there? If you're disabled, are there facilities to help you?

Although you don't usually have much control over the room, you might be able to choose the type of seating for your audience and the furniture on the platform. There are several options:

- theatre style
- classroom
- U-shaped/amphitheatre
- boardroom.

For any group larger than 25 people, *theatre-style* seating is the most appropriate. The platform from which you will be speaking will usually be higher than your audience. The *Classroom* layout, as the name suggests, lends itself to tutorial-type presentations, where you will probably have a desk or table facing the group who will each have their own writing surface. This arrangement is ideal for teaching, but not very satisfactory if you're giving a lecture to a large audience or want to create a more intimate atmosphere. You will be at the centre of the proceedings with a *U-shaped/amphitheatre* arrangement but this time your audience will be seated informally around you. This works well for staff meetings or something similar. The long rectangular table of a *boardroom* arrangement can be very intimidating. If you have to address a group of people seated in this way, make sure that you present from either end, not at the side, although No. 10 Downing Street obviously disagrees – the Prime Minister traditionally sits at the centre of the long side of table when chairing Cabinet meetings.

Let the organisers know in good time what stage furniture you will need. For instance, the author Edward de Bono, originator of the concept of 'lateral thinking', always gives his lectures sitting down. He is, I am told, very particular about the type of chair he uses. My quality test at conference venues is the provision of good-quality peppermints; decanters filled with lurid lime or orange cordial don't impress me. Props, visual aids or furniture only become a problem if you haven't thought about them in advance.

What should you wear?

Whatever you wear when you're speaking in public should be viewed as a costume, as part of your performance (see Chapter 9). At this stage, the only important thing is to establish what everyone else will be wearing, so that you can plan.

Who will be in the chair?

Apart from the audience, the chairperson is your most important contact. Fall foul of him or her and you could find yourself side-tracked very quickly. Even if you aren't asked to, it's always sensible to provide the chairperson with a very brief biography and witty personal anecdote to help him/her introduce you. This text must be written in conversational style and you must read it aloud before sending it.

Make yourself as available as you can. Chairpeople seem to enjoy and have time for meetings. You won't be expected to go to all of them, but try and attend at least one; this will ensure that the chairperson recognises you on the day. Sometimes there won't be preliminary meetings, in which case I would suggest making contact by phone, fax or e-mail prior to the event, and personal contact just before the programme starts. These preparatory meetings often create valuable opportunities for you to affect the way the programme is to be run.

Who are the other speakers?

Just as it pays to research your audience (see Chapter 3), so it does your fellow speakers. You will be surprised how few people take the trouble to make contact with other participants prior to an event. Doing so not only shows good manners, but also discreetly puts you in the driving seat. Asking that simple question could avoid the potential embarrassment of two people saying the same thing, with one perhaps saying it more persuasively than the other.

In what order will the speakers participate?

No one likes to be allotted the 'graveyard slot' immediately after lunch. If you're not able to influence the timing of your appearance, make a virtue of necessity and convince yourself that your presentation will be so effective it won't matter.

If you have the confidence you can exploit your disadvantage. I mentioned speaking at a Caribbean Tourism Conference where I was the last 'turn' of the day. People were tired and hot and beginning to fret about their journey home. I decided the humorous approach was the most appropriate:

> Ladies and gentlemen good evening. Despite the hour, look on
> the bright side. I am the only thing that stands between you and
> a rum punch – and I will make that wait as short as possible. ...

How long will your speech be?

The length of time you are asked to talk can vary enormously. If
you are asked to make a keynote speech, you might well be
expected to talk for 30–45 minutes. On the other hand, if you are
one of three speakers introducing a workshop session, ten minutes
will be quite long enough.

Essentially it doesn't matter how long you've been given, so long
as you know beforehand and can plan accordingly (see Chapter 4).

Will there be visual aids?

This potentially controversial topic deserves a chapter to itself and
is given one at Chapter 7. At an early stage of information
gathering, it is enough to establish what equipment will be
available, and whether you will be expected to operate it.

Will there be sound or autocue facilities?

Thankfully the days of the howl-back in-house sound system are
almost a thing of the past. You should establish whether you will
need to use a microphone and, if so, what kind. Don't forget to ask
if you will be expected to use an autocue and, if so, whether it is on
one or two screens.

Will there be a height-adjustable lectern?

It's a small point, but it saves a great deal of embarrassment and
awkwardness if you establish beforehand whether you are likely to
need an adjustable lectern. Too high and you'll suffer as H.M. The
Queen did on a trip to Washington (where only the tips of her
spectacles and hat were visible); too low, and you're in danger of
not being able to read your notes or cue cards.

Will there be questions from the floor?

Inexperienced speakers often feel very threatened by the prospect of spontaneous questions, mainly because they fear they will be made to look inadequate if they don't know the answers. So long as you know your subject and have anticipated what you're likely to be asked, there is no need to be intimidated. In fact, you could look on question time as one of the most stimulating aspects of the meeting.

Will your presentation be recorded?

It is odd what a paralysing effect a video camera or cassette recorder can have on a speaker. However, the fact that your words of wisdom are to be committed to (at least short-term) history shouldn't make any difference to your performance.

Will the media be there?

Most speakers tend to look on the media as alien, and they are invariably unnerved at the thought of their presence. This neurosis is understandable, but unnecessary if the speakers know what to expect and how to deal with them (see Chapter 11).

Should you provide copies of your presentation, or other publicity material?

It's common practice for politicians to make the text of their speeches available, and people who attend conferences – particularly if they've paid for the privilege – seem to expect a copy of notes and slides. These might be irksome to produce, but they can be a valuable marketing tool.

People often agree to take part in a conference because of the potential publicity value. Whatever benefits might accrue, I'm not in favour of distributing publicity brochures like confetti: I have found that it is far more effective to exchange business cards and follow up a connection by letter or phone call.

Will you be expected to stay on after the presentation?

There are no fixed rules of etiquette about whether you should stay on after your presentation. On the whole, if you can make the time, it's better to accept the invitation. If you do stay, don't forget you're still on duty.

Is the audience being charged admittance and will you charge a fee?

It is important to know whether your audience is fee-paying. There is an argument that an audience feels it is getting better value if it has been charged admittance. As far as your presentation is concerned, it shouldn't make any difference to your degree of preparation or your level of performance.

Whether or not *you* should ask for a fee depends very much on the situation. There is a lucrative after-dinner speaking circuit, where celebrities can charge several thousand pounds for a witty speech; however, most people usually accept that giving a presentation or making a speech can be of mutual benefit and therefore only ask for travel and out-of-pocket expenses. If I had to stay overnight, I would certainly ask for my hotel expenses to be reimbursed.

➡ WHAT NEXT?

If you have diligently asked all these questions, you are now ready to turn your attention to your particular audience.

Chapter 3
Your audience

'The play was a great success, but the audience was a total failure.'

(Oscar Wilde, after the first performance of *Lady Windermere's Fan*)

Giving an effective presentation is reliant on three interdependent aspects: audience, content and performance. Content and performance will be dealt with later. Let's for now concentrate first on your audience and its foibles.

Performing in front of an audience can be very seductive. Establishing a good rapport quickly promotes a sense of well-being and power. It gives a giddy sensation to hear a group laugh at a wry observation or gasp at an unusual fact. And applause is one of the most gratifying responses in the human repertoire. Unfortunately, not many people who give speeches enjoy these spin-offs, usually because they have failed to appreciate that the success of a speech is as much to do with understanding the audience and meeting its expectations as it is with giving an energetic performance.

The show-business fraternity is a master of 'audience control'. Look how comics 'work' a crowd, either by hurling insults or compliments from the stage or, sometimes, actually physically joining them. They know the importance of audience involvement and they know how to get it, often incorporating that enviable technique of making each member of the audience feel he is the only person the entertainer is talking to. Most of us might wince at the show-business habit of complimenting an audience on *its* performance at the end of a show, but it is worth remembering that the way an audience performs will often be a direct mirror of your own performance.

One dictionary definition of an audience is a 'group of listeners or spectators'. There are, of course, a wealth of possibilities within that bald description. Audiences can be unpredictable, prone to mood swings, inattentiveness and sometimes outright anarchy. They also have a limited attention span. But one rule germane to *all* audiences, whatever their size, is that they should be treated with *respect*.

It is not uncommon, especially if the speaker has been allotted the 'graveyard' slot after lunch, to have members of any audience fall asleep. It happened once when I was addressing the Law Society. No amount of animated gesture or verbal pyrotechnics could keep a pink-faced gentleman in the front row awake. I soldiered on and resisted the temptation to use him as a catalyst for audience involvement. It is a realistic speaker who accepts that no audience will listen in rapt attention to the whole of his presentation. However willing, a listener will drift off into private reveries. It is estimated that most people can only listen for about five to ten minutes before retreating to a world of their own. As a speech continues, these concentration lapses become more frequent and result, after about an hour, in 'information overload'. The challenge for the speaker is to find ways of compensating for this involuntary behaviour.

It is useful to accept that there are good and bad times to give a presentation. People's intellectual sharpness varies during the day, in response to internal biological rhythms. According to Christopher Turk, author of *Effective Speaking* (Chapman & Hall, UK, 1985), both body temperature and hormone levels change in a rhythmic cycle. Most people, he says, are at their best in the morning, but some do not reach their peak until midday, or even during the afternoon. Body temperature and hormone levels tend to reduce during the mid-afternoon in all of us, and hence the need for the ubiquitous tea break (see Chapter 8).

The day of the week is also important. We've all heard people joke about a faulty car as having 'come off the Friday assembly line'. People really *are* tired at the end of a working week, just as they are less focused on a Monday after the weekend. It would seem, therefore, that the ideal time to speak, for maximum audience impact, is 10.30 a.m. on a Tuesday morning. The vast majority of presenters who aren't allotted this coveted slot, will be relieved to know that there are ways of ensuring audience attention at any time or day of the week.

➡ WHY IS YOUR AUDIENCE THERE?

People attend a presentation for many reasons, and these reasons are discussed below. They include:

- obligation
- to be entertained
- to learn
- to pass the time
- to network
- to impress
- to manipulate politically
- to burgle ideas.

The list may look intimidating, but it is important to come to terms with the different needs and motives of your audience. It is equally important not to be daunted by the challenge of trying to satisfy everyone. You might not please *all* of them *all* of the time but, if you know what most of them will like and what they won't, you will have a chance of keeping their attention.

Obligation

At some time in our lives, many of us are required to attend lectures, seminars or meetings at which we are forced to take a passive role. This sense of obligation sets up a potential resistance between us and the speaker: if we didn't have to be there, we could be doing something else. An intelligent speaker will know whether audience attendance is mandatory and may acknowledge the fact in his opening remarks.

To be entertained

Many organisations use speakers more for their entertainment than content value. Inviting a group of people to listen to someone talking is often a useful bonding tool, the message being of secondary importance. Large organisations often use celebrities to chair a conference or give the after-dinner vote of thanks. This device appeals to the aspirational in us all.

When thinking about your presentation, it is important to remember the need to entertain. A combination of nerves and a misguided belief that you will only be taken seriously if you behave seriously often results in the entertainment element of the speech getting buried. It is such a missed opportunity if you let this happen. There are many things you can do to add extra zest, which are discussed in Chapter 9.

To learn

Half the battle is won if you know that your audience is hungry for information. The other half, as I've already said, is being able to impart that information in an entertaining and memorable way. A string of unconnected or unintelligible facts will result in disappointment for both you and your audience.

To pass the time

Every potential speaker likes to think that an audience is there solely to listen to him. Unfortunately, this is not always the prime motivation. Attending a lecture is often an attractive way of passing the time. This shouldn't discourage a speaker, but be seen (and used) as an opportunity to surprise and convert.

To network

Anyone who has attended an industry conference knows that, for most delegates, the presentations tend to be secondary to the networking opportunities. Most of the important business is done between seminars rather than during them. This shouldn't deter you from taking your presentation seriously; not only will there be some people in the audience interested in what you have to say, but also the spin-off benefits of your name appearing in the conference agenda and post-conference reports will be invaluable. There is also the possibility of media presence. Politicians will often agree to address the humblest of gatherings, in the knowledge that the real benefit will come from subsequent press coverage.

To impress

You mustn't be surprised if several members of your audience use the occasion of your speech not to listen and learn but as an arena in which to be noticed. This game plan doesn't usually become clear until question time, at which point the attention-seeking delegate will deliver a wordy dissertation disguised as a question or ask something deliberately obtuse to expose your lack of knowledge. Notes on handling questions are dealt with in Chapter 10.

To manipulate politically

Any organisation, be it a parish council, an FT 100 company or a voluntary playgroup committee, is quite likely to attract one or two politically motivated members. It is useful, therefore, to expect the presence of a few such people in any group you address. They will shamelessly sabotage your platform for the sake of scoring political points. As with the members of your audience who are there simply to be noticed, it is best to avoid rather than engage. An audience will soon tire of someone monopolising the floor and become even more sympathetic to you.

To burgle ideas

As there is really no such thing these days as a completely confidential exchange of ideas – even cabinet meetings are apparently no longer leak-free zones – there is a tough decision to be made about introducing new information and risking someone stealing your idea. Your initial research into the composition of your audience will probably give you some insight into that likelihood, but the old maxim, 'if in doubt, keep it out' should be applied if you are genuinely anxious about copyright infringement.

➡ THINGS THAT ANNOY AN AUDIENCE

One of the most effective ways of avoiding some of the classic mistakes people make when speaking in public is to ask yourself what standard or level of competence you yourself expect when you are in an audience. Just as everyone these days is an armchair television critic, so all of us are able to judge the quality of a presentation. Having yawned, scratched and fidgeted my way through innumerable presentations, I set out below a summary of habits and affectations that most audiences find irritating, and then discuss them in further detail. They are:

- apologetic from the start
- lack of preparation – the 'early draft' syndrome
- misjudgment of the audience
- inappropriate use of visual aids
- unskilled use of technology
- inaudibility
- speeding through
- absence of signposting
- lateness
- overrunning
- sending a substitute speaker
- deviation from the published subject
- unoriginality
- jargon
- self-promotion
- regional bias (or lack of it)
- lack of performance

Apologetic from the start

There is nothing more disappointing than a speaker whose opening statment contains an apology: 'I shouldn't really be giving this talk. So, you'll have to forgive me if I appear to lose my way sometimes ...' (so, why are you?); 'I'm sorry I'm late; the traffic, you know ...' (the traffic is always bad around that time).

Lack of preparation – the 'early draft' syndrome

The one overriding inadequacy that most irritates an audience is lack of preparation. There are a number of give-away phrases: 'I should really have edited this list down but, you know how it is ...'; 'I see that we're running out of time here, which is a pity, as the main point I wanted to make was ...'; 'I wasn't able to get precise figures to back up my argument, but I hope you'll accept that ...'.

If a speaker doesn't know where he or she is heading, how can an audience be expected to follow? A consequence of this ill-preparedness is, not surprisingly, uncertain delivery and mutual evaporation of confidence. An audience quickly loses interest in unfocused presentations and soon shows its unease.

Misjudgment of the audience

Although performing in public tends to stimulate egotistical needs, it is important, if you are to communicate effectively, to think not in terms of what *you* will get out of the experience but how your *audience* will benefit. If you adopt this approach, you'll avoid several audience-alienating pitfalls.

- parading your intelligence by littering your speech with esoteric Latin quotations
- dropping names
- going off at tangents
- insulting your audience by assuming they are at best ill-informed and at worst stupid – they will be neither.

Inappropriate use of visual aids

Very few speech-writers will admit that the use of a visual aid is more for their use than for the benefit of the audience. A visual aid can be a valuable asset, but ony if it is there genuinely to guide the audience. The speaker who uses his visual aids purely as his script runs the risk of losing his audience altogether.

Unskilled use of technology

Audiences expect a speaker to be able to use technology, and they don't expect it to be used apologetically. One wrongly inserted 35mm slide is forgivable; two, to paraphrase Oscar Wilde, suggests carelessness. The ubiquitous overhead projector, still the most popular visual aid, is the piece of equipment that seems to cause the most problems: the sight of a speaker trying inexpertly to separate sheets of acetate and place them correctly on the glass surface guarantees loss of audience confidence. Activating a video machine or cassette recorder is another technical hazard zone, as is the latest innovation, the self-operated computer-generated graphic.

Mumbled apologies about not being very good with technology do not go down well. *If you are going to use equipment make sure it works and you know how to operate it.*

Inaudibility

Inaudibility is one of the most frequent reasons given for provoking audience displeasure. And in these days of sophisticated audio technology, being born with a soft voice isn't a credible excuse. If you know you speak softly, always ask for a microphone.

Speeding through

Most inexperienced speakers don't realise that it takes much more concentration to abstract meaning from the spoken word than it does from the written. You don't have the advantage of being able to go at your own pace and retrace your steps for clarification. That is why speaking at the wrong speed is one of the quickest ways of alienating your audience.

I once worked with a client on a speech which, on the first run-through, was too long. On instruction that this problem must be addressed, he dutifully withdrew and returned a short time later to re-present. The speech did indeed take less time to deliver. It wasn't shorter, he had simply speeded up.

Absence of signposting

Unless the speaker is aware of the need to identify different parts of the speech and signpost changes in direction, his audience will quickly become confused and ultimately switch off.

Lateness

An audience doesn't like to be kept waiting. Expectancy is at its peak just before the start of a presentation and it would be a pity to sacrifice such focused attention by starting late. Apart from anything else, it is bad manners. The only way to ensure you don't experience the (even psychological) 'slow handclap' of a frustrated audience is to put punctuality high up your list of presentation priorities.

Overrunning

Although hard to believe, most audiences like to be controlled and like to follow an agenda. Just as they sense a breakdown in control if a speaker is late, so they react if someone goes over his allotted time. An inability to keep to a timetable reduces an audience's confidence in a speaker and consequently acceptance of his message. Although not usually a conscious criticism of poor time-keeping, when audiences are questioned about the performance value of a presentation, many will condense their feelings into phrases such as 'he bored the pants off me, he just droned on and on'. There is also the irritating knock-on effect caused by an undisciplined speaker, namely the forcing of subsequent speakers to change or edit their speeches at the last minute.

Sending a substitute speaker

An audience will feel very let down of it is asked to make do with a substitute speaker. Naturally, there are occasions when the reason for a 'no show' is legitimate, but a cynical audience will be hard to placate. If you are in *any* doubt that you might not be able to meet your obligation, don't accept the invitation.

Conversely, if you happen to be the luckless substitute, then have the confidence to make a plus out of the situation and lighten the mood with humour.

Deviation from the published subject

It is a foolhardy spokesperson who veers too widely from the advertised content of his presentation. Not even a celebrity speaker can expect to get away with a poorly constructed presentation. Doing so will imply that the speaker hasn't considered a particular audience important enough to warrant diligent preparation. Equally irritating is the presenter who overlaps the content of someone else's speech. This is quite different from reinforcing a point made in a previous presentation, a technique which can help unite an audience in a common theme.

Unoriginality

Although everyone will accept that points being made may have been made before, it will react badly if the speaker hardly bothers to disguise the fact that he's simply recycling information. Audiences also always feel short-changed by speakers who appear to be giving a speech they have presented before. Nor do they respond well to tired old jokes.

Jargon

Like visual aids, jargon can be used as a crutch, but you use them thus at your peril when addressing an audience. To use a different analogy, jargon is the weed in the garden of language; it is prolific and very difficult to get rid of, but get rid of it you must if you're to communicate effectively.

The rule is very simple: if your audience isn't likely to understand it, don't use it.

Self-promotion

No one in an audience will be impressed by a speaker's attempt to bolster self-esteem by constant name dropping. Credibility will have been established either in programme notes or by whoever makes the introductions; there is thus no need to keep reminding the audience of your qualifications. An attitude of modesty rather than conceit wins over an audience every time.

Most audiences understand and will accept the tacit relationship that exists between it and a speaker. In return for imparting useful information in an entertaining way, it will allow a degree of self-promotion. In a promotional media interview, for example, in return for turning up and filling pages or airtime, the interviewee's name, title and company will always be mentioned, sometimes both at the beginning and end of the interview. But if a speaker goes beyond the protocol of, say, two mentions of his new book, an audience will – as one – begin to smell a promotional rat and subsequently lose interest.

Regional bias (or lack of it)

One way of spotting a presentation taken 'off the shelf' and (maybe) dusted down is the absence of any regional references. For instance, a talk on volcanoes probably has universal appeal, but it would be insensitive not to refer to a country's own volcano. Similarly, an after-dinner speech given at a local cricket club would not be well received if the only anecdotes were about the England national side.

Lack of performance

An audience, quite rightly, expects something in return for its passive participation in a presentation. Ideally, it wants to be entertained. Anyone who accepts that challenge, therefore, has also to accept that, for the duration of the presentation, he or she must be looked upon as a performer. To this end, no presenter must ever assume that he or she can get away with simply reading a text. There must be an impression of spontaneity, energy and enthusiasm.

A speaker must also recognise that physical rigidity is almost as off-putting as a speech delivered with no variety of pitch, pace or volume. A speaker might feel more secure by standing statue-still, but the audience will quickly tire and begin to look for other visual diversions. Just as disconcerting is the speaker who cannot keep still.

➡ LESSONS FROM A BAD EXAMPLE

It's an unlucky audience that has to sit through a presentation littered with any or all of those delivery disasters, but I recently attended a seminar that came uncomfortably close. It was billed as an opportunity to debate the commercial potential of the Internet, and we were promised three speakers, all at the cutting edge of new technology. Not unreasonably, we assumed the visual back-up would be equally futuristic.

The first speaker was an editor of a magazine published on the Internet. Unfortunately, something had happened to his lap-top between leaving his office and hailing a cab. Consequently, we were subjected to a halting presentation, made all the worse for constant apologies, illustrated with kindergarten overheads most of which he obscured by his position. Had he made light of the problem, the audience would have shared his misfortune and made allowances; instead, his lack of composure and constant apologies made us uneasy and I spent most of the time counting how often he dropped his acetates, apologised, or stood in front of the projector. Such a pity, and such a waste of an opportunity. Three lessons can be learned from that experience:

- Check and re-check the computer.
- Have back-up cue cards with an outline of your speech.
- Sloppy overheads are worse than no overheads at all.

Our second speaker's computer-generated graphics were working satisfactorily, to the audible relief of the audience. It became quickly apparent, however, that he hadn't rehearsed. As a result, each change of graphic seemed as much of a surprise to him as it was to us. He also didn't realise that if something is self-evident, it isn't necessary to talk the audience through it. Finally (although I am in favour of keeping graphics as simple as possible), he certainly hadn't made full use of the software with which he could have created much more visually arresting images than he did. There are again three lessons to be learned:

- Rehearse with graphics.
- Make sure the graphics are relevant.
- Make maximum use of software.

The third speaker potentially had the best approach of all. Defying expectation, he announced he wouldn't be using any visual aids. True to his word, he didn't use a single slide, overhead, video or flipchart. Barely looking up, he read his speech at break-neck speed with no inflection, pitch or pace, and it was over-filled with statistics that no one was given the time to absorb. As a result, many of the fascinating things he had to say about future uses of the Internet were lost in a sea of undiluted words. The three lessons to be learned are thus:

- All speeches require verbal 'white space', signposting, pace, pitch and pause.
- Eye contact with an audience is essential.
- Presentations must be written to be spoken, not read.

➡ WARNING SIGNALS FROM YOUR AUDIENCE

How does an audience let you know when it's losing its patience? There are several early-warning signals. Even an inexperienced speaker will know when he has caught the attention of an audience. Although almost intangible, a speaker will be able to feel the participation of the group as a whole. Conversely, a presenter will instinctively know when she is beginning to lose them.

People behave differently in an audience from how they do when in small groups. Most people, especially in a work environment, accept the protocols of communication: you knock on doors before entering; you don't interrupt; and you certainly don't walk out on someone. An audience, on the other hand, if it collectively senses that it is not getting what it wants, will get restless and you will recognise their unease in the following four ways, discussed below:

- withdrawal of eye contact
- throat clearing, coughing and yawning
- restlessness
- heckling or walking out.

Withdrawal of eye contact

The first early-warning signal is a withdrawal of eye contact. If an audience is made to feel uncomfortable, it will try to avoid eye contact with the speaker. People will start gazing out of windows, looking at their feet or their watches or at each other. As I have already warned, the ultimate expression of visual excommunication is the member of the audience who falls asleep half-way through a presentation.

Throat clearing, coughing and yawning

An outbreak of throat clearing, coughing or yawning is another key indicator of audience unrest. Ten minutes earlier a silent hall, the auditorium is soon sounding like a doctor's mid-winter surgery. There is no proof that yawns signal boredom, and they may simply be the result of a stuffy room and a reflex response to the body's need for oxygen; however, like coughs and throat clearing, yawns are a signal of unease and very catching!

Restlessness

Restlessness is also evidence of disquiet. For no discernible reason, people start shuffling their feet, moving their chairs or dropping papers.

Heckling or walking out

The most tangible sign of tension or displeasure is when an individual deliberately tries to sabotage a meeting by either heckling or walking out. This is unlikely to happen to you if you write and deliver a good speech.

➡ **WHAT NEXT?**

The next chapter will help you formulate your ideas and put them into an easily remembered structure. This will help get you started so that you present your material in a manner that holds your audience's attention and communicates well with it.

Chapter 4
Think before you write

Health warning: only talk about subjects you understand.

Some of the best, if irreverent, speeches that I have heard have been made by best men at weddings. They succeed for two reasons: they know their subject well, and the audience is guaranteed to be responsive.

If you try to write and give a presentation on an unfamiliar subject, you are taking a terrible risk with your reputation as a public speaker and several rather unpleasant things could happen to you:

- The research will take too long and you may miss the point.
- The structure and writing won't come easily.
- When you come to present, your lack of confidence in your subject will tie you to your text and you'll read rather than talk.
- Eye contact with your audience will be minimal.
- You'll be uneasy about answering questions.

The net result will be that the audience will quickly see through you and your credibility will be severely dented.

However, you are unlikely to be asked to talk on an unfamiliar subject. Your problem is far more likely to be the fact that you know *too much* about your topic, rather than too little, and run the risk of drowning your audience in detail.

So, let's assume that you've accepted an invitation to talk to a group on a subject you know. As outlined in the previous chapters, you've already taken two important steps: you know why you have been invited, and you understand the type of audience you will have. Before you settle down to take your first tentative attempts at writing, it is useful to revisit some of that initial research, particularly the work you did on establishing your audience's expectations. Are they looking to be motivated, educated, scolded or cajoled? Appreciation of those expectations will guide you in the *tone* of what you say and thereby influence the content.

➡ GETTING STARTED: THINKING AROUND THE SUBJECT

Writers often report on the paralysing effect a blank sheet of paper or an empty PC screen has on their powers of composition. It is not the blank screen or empty sheet of paper that's to blame, it is insufficient preliminary *thinking* work. Unless you've really wrestled with your subject, no amount of paper-staring will get the speech written.

Certainly, before I penned the first sentence of this book, I burnt out a good number of brain cells mentally testing out ideas. My initial and primary preoccupation was to try to discover whether I could contribute anything new to a subject already thoroughly aired. If so, could I clearly and simply identify what that contribution would be? Had the book got a central theme? Was I going to write solely about presentation techniques or should I include a section on structuring and composition as well? Would the reader share my fascination in discovering whether what we eat or drink can affect our performance? It was only by addressing these questions in written form that I began to test whether a collection of random thoughts could be assembled into a framework that would form the basis of a book.

The first step in this testing period was to write a *synopsis*: in this instance, it was a 250-word summary of what the book was about. I followed this with a detailed treatment, which consisted of chapter headings and content bullet points. It was a difficult process and required discipline, made all the more frustrating by a desire to get started on the text. But no publisher would even consider an idea, let alone commission a book, without being able to read something that gave them confidence that I knew where I was going.

Although writing a speech is not nearly as daunting as promising to deliver several thousand words of typescript for publication, the same principles of discipline and mental preparation must be applied. Your subject, synopsis and 'chapter' headings *must* come before you start writing the text.

Don't panic. If you allow yourself time and space, ideas *will* come and you will be able to shape them into a presentation. Try to get into a state of 'mental free-fall'. This is the time in your life when you can legitimately day-dream. Even though you've got a deadline, go and mow the lawn, tidy the airing cupboard or put up a shelf. While your body is active, your mind will be free to wander. Combining the practical with the mental will also eradicate any guilt pangs you might feel if you are caught in so selfish a state as leaning on the garden gate rather than oiling it!

People who use more of the right side of their brain find the initial stages of presentation planning easier than those who use the left. This is simply because the right side of the brain favours creative, broad-brush thinking and the left side logical, detailed thought. Even if you know your mental strengths lie in precise, logical thought, it is still possible to draw upon the artistic, random, right-hand side of the brain and apply lateral-thinking techniques pioneered by Edward de Bono.

In his book, *The Mechanism of Mind* (Jonathan Cape, UK, 1969), de Bono talks about 'undoing selection processes':

> Lateral thinking seeks to avoid the selecting processes of natural thinking and logical thinking in order to find out whether a useful arrangement has been excluded by such selection processes. Thus no attention is paid to either the negative blocking of logical thinking or the dominant attraction of natural thinking selection. In logical thinking each step must be justified, otherwise it would be blocked with a negative. In lateral thinking the steps do not have to be justified ... it seems to break down the natural self-selection of cliché units or patterns that have been built up on the memory-surface. It may be a matter of cutting across these units and re-creating new units. It may be a matter of distorting an obvious pattern in order to let a new one emerge. Anything that is fixed, accepted or taken for granted can be re-examined in an attempt to set free

the information imprisoned within it or to remove the blocking effect it might be having.

I have seen de Bono explain his theory in person. I was at one of his lectures during which he convinced a group of apparently bored middle managers that it was possible to discard a rigid train of thought to find solutions to problems. With skilful use of an overhead projector and some coloured pens, he taught us how to use random ideas to formulate a thought pattern that, if taken to its limits, could lead to some unexpected conclusions. His limited drawing skills, if anything, added to the impact of his thesis.

➡ JUDGING THE DURATION

Before you can begin being creative, one of the first things to be done is to review how long you're going to speak for (you should have discovered your allotted time early on – see Chapter 2).

The Zulu leader Chief Mangosuthu Buthelezi is in the *Guinness Book of Records* for having given the longest speech ever. He addressed the KwaZulu legislation assembly and spoke for eleven days, averaging two-and-a-half hours each day. Closer to home, former Prime Minister William Gladstone subjected MPs to four-and-a-half hours of his thoughts. Fortunately, few of us will ever be called upon to either speak or listen for such a length of time, although a barrister colleague once boasted to me that his closing summary of a case lasted three hours – and, of course (see Chapter 1), Nelson Mandela's lasted for four. In contrast, the Queen's Christmas message is usually five to seven minutes.

Tradition has established accepted optimum lengths for most types of speeches. As a general rule, *no speech should be longer than 30 minutes*; human attention span simply isn't able to concentrate or absorb much information for anything longer. Whatever duration you decide, stick to it. Neither audiences nor fellow speakers will thank you for overrunning.

A very general guide to speech lengths is given in Checklist 4.1.

| Checklist 4.1 | **A guide to speech lengths** |

Duration (mins)	Type of speech
2–3	Accepting an award (shorter if possible)
	Opening a fête, supermarket etc.
	Chairman's welcome and close
	Vote of thanks
	Toast
	Panellist's speech
10	Funeral address
	Sermon (clergy please note)
	After-dinner speech
	Wedding speech
	Chairman's summary
20	Directors' reports at an AGM
	Keynote speech
30	Business pitch (usually including questions)
	Product launch (per participant)
60	Academic lecture

Knowing the length of your speech, you can now start thinking about its content.

➡ **ORDERING YOUR THOUGHTS**

I referred earlier to the stage of 'mental free-fall' in which, by thinking about your subject in an unrestrained way you will have generated many (not necessarily connected) ideas. The next step is to commit those thoughts to paper.

Suppose you have been invited to talk to your local Rotary Club about 'How new technology will change the way we communicate'. Where do you start? Firstly, go back to the brief and, just as you would an examination question, make sure you understand it. Analyse the title to produce the key elements that will form the basic structure and subject matter of your presentation. In this case, the two elements are:

New technology ... Effect on communication

Write these two headings in the centre of a piece of paper. On the rest of the paper scribble down, applying the technique of 'mental free-fall', any word that comes into your head associated with either of the two categories. For our example, the following list (in no particular order) might apply and should only take a very short time to compile:

- speed
- power
- electricity
- Bill Gates
- Sir Clive Sinclair
- direct banking
- Internet
- cable
- digital
- Windows
- DOS
- voice mail
- intranet
- virtual reality
- networking
- databases
- lasers
- lap-top
- Logie Baird
- binary
- CD-Rom
- cordless
- white
- video conferencing
- DNA
- imaging

With a little basic research, it would be possible to write a paragraph about each of these topics. For argument sake, let's assume you are going to write 300 words on each topic. There are 26 topics listed, resulting in 7,800 words of text. Someone speaking moderately fast covers about 170 words a minute. So, if you were to give each topic an equal amount of time, you would be speaking for at least 45 minutes – and that is not allowing for greetings, introductions, signposting, summaries, conclusions, anecdotes, repetition and farewells.

Clearly, then, however wedded you are to the list, you have got to become your own editor and begin to select. Although this list was genuinely random, I was intrigued, when I looked at it more closely, to discover that it seemed to be self-categorising, so that the random words could be grouped as A (conceptual), B (people) and C (specific).

A	B	C
speed	Logie Baird	lap-top
power	Bill Gates	voice mail
laser	Sir Clive Sinclair	Internet
digital		databases
electricity		video conferencing
white		CD-Rom
DNA		direct banking
imaging		intranet
networking		Windows
cordless		DOS
virtual reality		cable
binary		

You now have a list which offers up many choices to advance your central subject. Use this freedom, for it is *your* choice. You may choose to centre it around people and argue that it is only because of the contributions of such people as Logie Baird, Sir Clive Sinclair and Bill Gates that we are living through a technological revolution, and then elaborate your point by taking a key invention from each person to illustrate how our communication channels have been changed by technology. You may decide that the ability to digitalise sound and pictures is the most exciting aspect of new technology, in which case that topic would become the main focus of the presentation. Alternatively, you may look at the random list and see an Aladdin's cave of technological advancement, all of which have affected how we communicate. Why not take a specific environment – say the HQ of a manufacturing company with regional branch offices – and take your audience on a virtual tour around that office, pointing out the new technology as you go.

The choices thrown up by this 'mental free-fall' exercise should be liberating and challenging. It can sometimes be even more useful if you ask a colleague to work with you on this initial stage.

➡ WRITING SOMETHING DOWN

Now the real work begins. Don't worry about the *niceties* of writing at this stage; concentrate on what to say. Imagine you are writing to a bright, curious 14-year-old niece and you are describing to her your first experience of a video conference. You'll find that the text will be full of dashes, exclamation marks, phrases in brackets and the occasional liberties with grammar. Although it may look a little odd, this is *precisely* the style you should adopt when starting off: it will free you from a fixation with the printed word and allow you to 'hear' what you're writing.

One of my earliest jobs in television was as a researcher/writer for *This Is Your Life* and, amongst other things, it was my job to find original ways of saying 'and you thought he was in Australia, but he's not, he's here with us tonight' and to paraphrase the guests' stories not only to ensure that the programme ran to time but also so that they sounded natural. It is a discipline that has served me well and, if I were allowed to give only one piece of advice about writing presentations, *I would urge everyone to write as they speak not as they read*. I was recently helping an earnest young man with his presentation. All was going well until he came to the last paragraph when he said 'And, finally, before I depart, I would like …'. I couldn't resist the temptation of asking him what flowers I should send to his funeral. He got the point.

Everyone has their own preference, but I find, at this very early stage of writing, that it is easier to compose in longhand. Whichever format you select, write about 350 words towards your speech, colloquialisms and lazy grammar included, and then read it aloud. If it sounds right and makes sense, you have the makings of a good speech-writer.

This simple exercise will also have helped you set the *tone* of your presentation. The language will be yours, how you naturally communicate. You will, therefore, not sound as if you've borrowed someone else's script. To be convincing, you have to be confident, clear and in control, qualities that have nothing to do with the mythical attributes of successful public speaking.

➡ STRUCTURE

Now that you are warming to your subject, you must take into account the discipline needed to create the structure that will enable you, in Hillaire Belloc's famous words, to:

Tell them what you're going to tell them, then tell them, then tell them that you've told them.

Remember, too, that old adage 'less is more'. So few speakers appreciate how little an audience is able to absorb from a presentation. If they remember the beginning and the end, you will have done well. The problem is that intellectual vanity gets in the way of clarity. Instinctively, you are driven towards telling your audience every morsel about your carefully researched subject, regardless of its relevance. Trust me: verbal austerity wins every time.

Before you begin work on the structure, your piece of paper with the initial brief might look as shown in Figure 4.1.

What do we mean by structure? It is a method to take you safely from your opening remarks to your conclusion. There are many

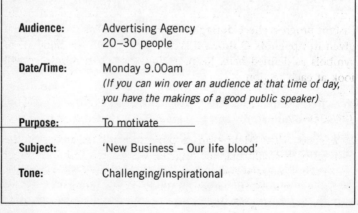

Audience:	Advertising Agency 20–30 people
Date/Time:	Monday 9.00am *(If you can win over an audience at that time of day, you have the makings of a good public speaker)*
Purpose:	To motivate
Subject:	'New Business – Our life blood'
Tone:	Challenging/inspirational

Figure 4.1: An initial brief

different ways to structure a speech. Some people opt for a kind of 'whodunnit' approach, telling a story, laying a few clues, eventually leading up to a dénouement or punch line. Others take a much more traditional chronological route. Some feel safer with a more legalistic style in which they posit an argument; back it up with evidence and slam home the conclusion.

All these methods have their merit but, for the purposes of this book, I have opted for the classical approach to speech writing, namely that each section of a presentation should be clearly identified. Adopting this method will ensure a logical sequence and allow ample opportunity to recap and summarise. I have called the sections, respectively:

- greeting (——)
- menu (●)
- housekeeping (▲)
- main body (▬)
- summary (■)
- conclusion (✚)

For each of the elements in my structure, I find it helpful to visualise them in symbolic form, as shown in the above list (although you can, of course, choose your own set of symbols). I then use the symbols to organise the material as I write, subsequently transferring them onto cue cards where they act as an instant progress check during my presentation. The sample speech given in Appendix C shows this in practice, with the same set of symbols as defined here. Keeping these points in mind, we will look at each section.

The greeting (——)

It was Dr Albert Mehrabian, a professor and researcher at the University of California, Los Angeles, who stated that only 7 per cent of any message is communicated with words, 38 per cent is relayed by voice (tone, accent, inflection, projection and so on) and the remaining 55 per cent is communicated by non-verbal body language. Couple those statistics with the observation that it takes the average person less than ten seconds to form an impression of someone, and you will appreciate how vitally important those opening moments of a presentation are.

Why is it that people find it so difficult to get a presentation off on the right note? Why do they shuffle onto a stage looking as if they are on the last walk to the electric chair? Are they simply too nervous to do anything else or perhaps simply unaware of the poor impression they are making? Before you utter a single word, you have to have the confidence to let the audience get a good look at you and you've got to look at them. Walk with confidence up to the platform and over to the lectern, award them with a winning smile, arrange your notes, switch on your overhead projector or lap-top, give your audience time to take in what may be illustrated, take a deep breath and begin with a warm, confident greeting:

> Good morning, ladies and gentlemen. I am honoured to be given time to share my thoughts with you today. As Bill said, my name is Peter POKISS and I am International Sales Director of Global Imprint Corporation, responsible for new business. Put that another way. I'm Peter Pokiss and it's my job that's on the line if I don't manage to persuade all of you in this hall this morning of the importance of new business to our company.

That greeting must be delivered without the use of a *single* note. It must be delivered with confidence and panache and must achieve its goal of engaging the audience from the outset. If your audience contains dignitaries, then use the required forms of address set out in Appendix B.

You can capitalise on a good start by adding an anecdote, which will warm the atmosphere and engage their curiosity. Broadcaster and writer Alistair Cooke has been a master at introducing apparently unrelated anecdotal material into his presentations. Just when you've given up on ever following the plot, he has led you gently through his personal mental maze to enlightenment. Nevertheless, it took him years to hone his very special skill and I advise inexperienced speech writers to use unrelated anecdote with caution. But something relevant, pithy and entertaining right at the top of a speech will serve you well.

Some people prefer jokes to anecdotes. As we all know, if you are wobbly on punch lines or are apt to lose the thread or can only remember saucy ones, don't try to tell them. Far better to describe something that happened to you that will relate to your audience.

The menu (●)

The menu is a summary of the content of the speech. Never assume just because members of your audience have an agenda in front of them that they know what you're going to talk about. It is essential, at this early stage of your presentation that you 'headline' it. For our example, consider:

> I've called my talk this morning 'New business – our life blood', and I intend to prove to you not only why new business has to be at the heart of our strategy in the future but also how well positioned we are to take up the challenge and what we'll be doing at Head Office in support.

In that 20-second menu, you have let your audience know what to expect. (See also Appendix C, sample speech.)

Housekeeping (▲)

Audiences aren't mind-readers; on the whole, they are a group of polite individuals who are prepared to listen to you talk. But they do like to know what's expected of them. Housekeeping notes satisfy this need. They should be brisk and to the point and should usually contain the following information:

- The intended length of your speech.
- Whether or not questions can be asked and at what stage. (Remind people always to give their name and company before asking their questions and, if appropriate, to wait for a microphone.)
- Whether or not hand-out material will be available.
- Whether or not refreshments will be served later.

It looks so obvious on the printed page but, now that you're aware of the need, you'll be disappointed the next time you attend a seminar and no one has the courtesy to bother with housekeeping.

Body of speech (■■)

However many points you decide to make in a presentation, each one must have a clear beginning, middle and end to it, and a smooth transition from one point to the next. Remember that your audience will only absorb a limited amount of information and it may be beneficial to limit your speech to, at most, three key points. It will not only make you focus but will keep your audience's interest as well.

There may well be, of course, a few detours you want to take. There is no problem with that, just so long as they are neatly woven into your presentation. In that way your audience won't be confused about significance. Don't forget, though, that each key point should have a beginning, middle and end and contain a statement of the idea/argument/proposition, followed by detailed support of it, rounding off with a mini-summary and an indication of what comes next.

Bridging is a vital ingredient of good speech-writing. *You* know where you're going, but the audience does not; so please tell it.

Summary (■)

No audience can ever give you its full attention, and you must allow them their 'nodding-off' time – which is why the summary is just as important as the menu at the opening. It doesn't need to be long. Remember, you have anyway been summarising and building on the main subject of the presentation in each of your sections. The purpose of this final summary is to reinforce your central message and lead people comfortably to your conclusion.

The conclusion (+)

It is astonishing how bad the British are at finishing things. Have you noticed how difficult we find it to end a telephone conversation or leave a meeting? Ending a speech also seems to present the same problems. Just as with the greeting, it has to be tackled confidently and directly. You're the conductor; you're in charge; tell us what's going on. Thus, in our example:

> Ladies and gentlemen, I'm getting discreet signals from your Chairman, which either means he's ready for the refreshments, or he thinks I've gone on long enough. Either way, thank you all for listening. I hope we can continue the debate over coffee or, if anyone has any immediate questions, I'd be delighted to take them now. May I remind you to wait for the microphone, give your name and organisation and then ask your question. Thank you.

➡ TIMING

As a guideline and to help you calculate how many words you need to write, 160–170 words represent about a minute of spoken text. A single A4 sheet of text, with $1\frac{1}{2}$-line spacing and 14-point font, equals about two minutes' worth of speech; thus on average, a 15-minute speech will be about seven A4 pages with that layout. These calculations must only be taken as an *average*. Layout could affect timing and number of pages, as could the rate of your delivery. The only way to be completely accurate on timing is, of course, to rehearse it from beginning to end.

It is interesting to note that you can afford to talk a little more slowly when addressing a live audience than when a speech is being video'd. The loss of the physical and emotional relationship between speaker and audience (unless you're very experienced), flattens your video performance and requires you to speed up to compensate for the loss of interaction.

If you have the equipment available, it is very useful to film your presentation during reheasal. Apart from amusing your work colleagues, it will very quickly show you whether you're going at the right pace and whether your body language is effective.

And a final word of advice about writing a speech – remember two things: always leave an audience wanting more, and what you leave out can be as important as what you include. Willie Gavin, media planner for US ex-President Nixon, said (as quoted in J. McGinnis, *The Selling of the President*, 1969):

What you leave unsaid becomes what the audience brings to it. Lead 'em to the brink of the idea, but don't push across the brink. It's not the words, but the silences where the votes lie.

A useful final check to reassure yourself that you have written a clear presentation is to try to define the content in less than 30 seconds. If you can, you know where you are going.

➡ WHAT NEXT?

In the next chapter you will start refining your speech by learning how to avoid verbal pitfalls.

Chapter 5
Avoiding verbal pitfalls

By now, your research and mental discipline should be reaping its rewards. You know who your audience is and understand its expectations. You have a subject, a clearly defined path through the speech and a convincing close. Now is the time to be aware of some of the verbal pitfalls into which the inexperienced can fall.

How many times, when responding to a point, do you find yourself saying 'I see what you mean' rather than 'I hear what you mean' (although Americans do sometimes acknowledge a point by saying 'I hear you')? The unconscious use of the verb 'to see' suggests that we are creating a picture or pattern of understanding from what we have just heard, and this is a useful point to remember when giving a presentation.

➡ BAD HABITS TO AVOID

This is the stage of your preparation when it is useful to get the verbal and visual pitfalls out of the way. The following are bad habits to avoid:

- use of the royal 'we'
- over-politeness
- clichés
- acronyms
- jargon
- euphemisms

- foreign phrases
- diversions
- statistics
- jokes
- high-grade vocabulary
- bad language
- poor use of visual aids
- inaudability
- gimmicks

Further comments on each of them are set out below.

The royal 'we'

Speakers use the collective pronoun 'we' as some kind of uncon-scious safety net: 'It's not the kind of problem *we* normally have to deal with at the plant' suggests a shared responsibility. But how much more convincing if the speaker said 'It's not the kind of problem *I* normally have to deal with at the plant.' It's *your* speech, *your* audience. Take ownership of both, and have the courage to use the personal pronoun singular except where the 'we' refers to you and the audience combined ('We have all experienced ...'). Your audience will be instinctively grateful.

Over-politeness

The practice of appearing to plead for an audience's co-operation is an irritating trait. Isn't it a little insincere to appear to be seeking your audience's compliance? For example:

> We'd like this morning, if we may, to take you through what led
> up to the change of circumstances. We know it's been difficult,
> but we hope you'll agree, we cannot shirk our responsibilities.

By simply changing the personal pronoun and adopting a direct, rather than a falsely optional approach, the audience will immedi-ately know the speaker's intention:

This morning I'm going to take you through what has led to the change of circumstances. I know, and you know, things have been very difficult – and, together, we have to face up to our responsibilities.

Clichés

We are all guilty of littering our conversation with clichés. Hardly surprising that such conversational laziness finds its way into speech-writing. Grammatically and linguistically, there's nothing fundamentally wrong with the following text; it's simply paralysingly banal because of its overuse of tired old clichés and lack of original vocabulary.

I'm not going to beat about the bush because, at the end of the day and at this moment in time, when all's said and done (not to put too fine a point on it), the fact of the matter is that this is a hands-on, high-profile, ongoing situation between two people who are as different as chalk and cheese.

Acronyms

Everybody inside the BBC (British Broadcasting Corporation) knows that 'DG' refers to the Director General and an 'FM' is a Floor Manager, not a radio waveband; but outsiders wouldn't know what is being referred to. Food manufacturers are always referring to 'FMCGs' (fast-moving consumer goods). RIBA is The Royal Institute of British Architects; if not made clear at the start of your presentation, your audience might be forgiven for thinking you were about to launch into a Latin American song! The simple rule with regard to acronyms is to give them their full meaning at the beginning of a speech and to use the abbreviation thereafter.

Jargon

Jargon can be the weed in the garden of language.
Jargon can sometimes serve a useful function as verbal shorthand, but over-reliance has meant that it has become the scourge of

business communicators. I have collected some classics over the years, as given in Checklist 5.1.

Checklist 5.1   Jargon and its real meaning

- 'home category managers' – housewives
- 'control the dialogue' – be in control
- 'optimisation of penetration levels' – getting more business
- 'brand architecture' – creating an identity for a product
- 'small-ticket value' – inexpensive
- 'flex the product' – get customers to buy
- 'strategic corridors' – marketing plans
- 'apparel garments' – underwear
- 'seat at the table' – up there with the competition
- 'dimensionalise' – focus
- 'front-loaded activity' – focused marketing
- 'household penetration' – getting through to domestic consumers
- 'mission statement' – company objectives

Euphemisms

The British love their euphemisms.

- 'This really is rather a poor show' – You're fired.
- 'He's just popped out for a moment' – He's late and we don't know when he'll be in.
- 'I'm afraid our accounts department is closed for the afternoon' – I have no intention of paying you this week.

The British also have a tendency to use complicated rather than simple words:

- 'thought-provoking' – interesting
- 'problematical' – difficult

- 'indefatigable' – hard-working
- 'effervescent' – lively.

Sue Stapely, in her book *Media Relations for Lawyers* (The Law Society, UK, 1996), is a keen advocate of using simple language:

'clients'	use 'people'
'litigation'	use 'court cases'
'judiciary'	use 'judges'
'conveyancing'	use 'the legal side of buying and selling your home'
'administration of estate'	use 'putting someone's affairs in order after they die'.

Foreign phrases

The fear of not being appreciated is almost as great as that of being found to be intellectually wanting. This is why many speeches are peppered with foreign phrases. If you know your audience will understand the foreign phrase and the English alternative isn't as effective, then by all means use it; but *don't* do it simply to impress.

Sue Stapely rightly took me to task during a media training session with lawyers when I injected many superfluous Latin phrases into my questions. I was obviously trying to show off – a silly thing to do in view of the risk I ran in choosing the wrong phrase from my extremely limited legal lexicon and alienating the audience who wouldn't have understood. Some gratuitous foreign phrases to be used with caution are listed in Checklist 5.2

Checklist 5.2   Foreign phrases to use sparingly

- *persona non grata*
- *quid pro quo*
- *bona fide*
- *non sequitur*
- *inter alia*
- *ex gratia*

- *de rigeuer*
- *je ne sais quoi*
- *tempus fugit*

If, after the above warnings, you are still wedded to using a particular phrase, offer a rough translation as well.

Diversions

Alistair Cooke, mentioned earlier, has been one of the few broadcasters who has made a profession out of successfully using diversions. Inexperienced speech-givers do so at their peril.

The written and spoken word are two different creations. A reader can follow a fairly complicated sentence structure, and can always re-read for clarification, but with an audience you have no such leeway. Text written for speech, rather than to be read, needs to be more colloquial and must have both long and short sentences. How many times have you longed to help a speaker out when he loses his way in the middle of a long and complicated sentence? Don't risk the same embarrassment yourself by over-complicating your speech or indulging in diversions.

And don't get diverted from the need to make only one point at a time. I always refer to the occasion when I was interviewing a particularly self-important Minister for the Arts. In response to a genuinely information-seeking question, he pronounced that there were three ways to answer. He managed the first with typical political aplomb. There was a slight pause during which he sought for the second, followed immediately by the rolling of his eyeballs, the tell-tale sign of memory-loss. Pretending not to notice his awkward state I asked, 'And the third point Minister?' He did have the grace to admit defeat.

Diversions should not be confused with anecdotes. A diversion will often confuse and seldom add to the text, whereas an anecdote will illustrate and embellish.

Statistics

'There are three kinds of lies: lies, damned lies, and statistics' (from

The Pan Dictionary of Famous Quotations (Pan Books, UK, 1989)). According to the Oxford English Dictionary, statistics are 'numerical facts systematically collected', and, not surprisingly, they serve as a useful ally in written studies or reports.

However, they should be treated more cautiously in presentations. An audience has great difficulty in absorbing columns of figures or overcomplicated graphs, and so they should only be used when no alternative will give as clear a picture. A striking single phrase or statistic is often sufficient, as these examples on smoking-related risks demonstrate:

- 'Every ten seconds another person dies as a result of tobacco use.'
- 'Britain is known as the ASTHMA CAPITAL of Europe.'
- 'In the last fifty years, tobacco will have killed an estimated 20 million people in the European Union.'
- 'The World Health Organisation estimates there are approximately 1,100 million who smoke.'

Jokes

Laughter has an intoxicating effect on us all and is one of the quickest and most reliable ways of uniting audiences and speaker. Permission to laugh lowers tension and helps stimulate important interaction. But deciding how to make people laugh is often difficult.

Telling a joke would seem an obvious route. However, even though it is often the case that men tend to deliver the punchline of a joke better than women, only the most confident should include them in speeches. In all my years of making presentations, although always including an amusing remark early on to relax my audience, I have never had the confidence to either start or end with a formal joke.

Even worse is the inappropriate joke. What might go down well at an old boys' reunion would probably not be well received by a group of women attending a relaxation seminar.

High-grade vocabulary

> I put it to you. We're looking at a pusillanimous committee who
> can't or won't make a decision.

If, like me, you are drawn to the richness of the English language
and feel comfortable using words like 'pusillanimous', then use it.
But make sure that you invest the word with the right tone – in
this case disdain – so that the audience, even though they may not
understand the precise meaning of the word, will appreciate its
sentiment.

The wrong use of a word, a malapropism (named after Mrs
Malaprop in Sheridan's play *The Rivals*) can severely dent your
credibility. Not so critical, but often irritating to an audience, is the
all-too-frequent misuse of a word:

- infer/imply
- affect/effect
- complimentary/complementary
- disinterested/uninterested

The rule must be to use only those words whose meaning you
are sure of and, if you are unsure, to check up so as to avoid
embarrassing mistakes.

Bad language

Swearing is an expression of verbal distress. We all swear and by so
doing release pent up anger or frustration. Swearing in a presentation, however, doesn't work. Resorting to crude slang gives an
impression of loss of control. And you don't need to use it: 'I
bloody well won't let that happen to any one of you in this
audience today' can easily become 'I give you my solemn word
that I won't let that happen to any one of you in this audience
today'. If I was in that audience, I know which one I'd feel more
comfortable hearing.

Poor use of visual aids

A visual aid is principally there for your audience and not for you. It takes confidence not to use your visual aids as a personal crutch, and you mustn't. The least confident simply reproduce their speech on the acetates and veer irritatingly from script to screen, reading word-for-word. This is referred to as 'death by overhead' in public relations circles, and makes for a dull performance, at the same time ensuring that you have your back to your audience for a good proportion of the time.

The impenetrable visual aid can be equally irritating. What is the use of a slide that, unless explained, resembles nothing more than coloured sweets thrown onto glass?

The different types of visual aids and how to use them effectively will be discussed in Chapter 7. If you are not inclined to read further on this subject, bear in mind one useful acronym for all presenters: KISS – Keep It Simple, Stupid.

Inaudibility

If the audience cannot hear you, you will quickly lose its attention. With the availability of sophisticated microphone technology, there is no excuse for not being able to make yourself heard. Microphone technique is explained in Chapter 7.

If you haven't had time to test the acoustics of the room and there aren't any microphones in use, do a spot check with your audience before you begin by asking people in various parts of the room whether they can hear you. Techniques for raising the volume of your voice are dealt with in Chapter 8.

Gimmicks

It takes great confidence to carry off a gimmick throughout a presentation. For instance, if you decide to dress as Superman – to signal to your audience your ability to override all obstacles – then you've got to deliver your speech with as much, if not more, confidence than usual. The use of a simple prop, which will be discussed later, is usually much more effective and carries far less risk.

➡ WHAT NEXT?

With these warnings firmly in mind, now the fun starts and you can begin to build a presentation that people will enjoy and remember.

Chapter 6
Giving life to your speech

You've done a lot of basic work already. Now you can build in some refinements that will animate your text and help your delivery of it. What have you achieved so far? You know from the earlier chapters of this book, but the main points are thus:

- why you are there.
- audience make-up and expectations.
- length of speech and order of appearance.
- the venue.
- your subject matter, which can be defined in 30 seconds.
- the basic structure of your speech (with its coding by symbol as necessary).
    greeting (——)
    menu (●)
    housekeeping (▲)
    body of speech (▉▉)
    summary (■)
    conclusion (✚)
- bad habits to avoid.

Remember, the objective is to make a speech that will educate, inform and entertain. To achieve that end, William Gladstone, the British Liberal Prime Minister, had just six rules for successful speaking: simple words, short references, distinct diction, testing his argument beforehand, knowledge of the subject, and watching the audience.

➡ WEAPONS IN YOUR ARSENAL

Whilst all of these points are valid, there is a great deal more ammunition you can have in your arsenal. In this chapter, we shall look at the many other weapons you can employ to enhance your performance:

- a confident greeting
- the personal pronoun
- examples
- anecdotes
- quotations
- statistics
- humour
- repetition
- promises
- challenges
- rhetorical questions
- audience involvement
- good use of visual aids
- props

A confident greeting

According to Graham Lancaster, Chairman of an international public relations company, (Biss Lancaster), in his book *The 20% Factor* (Kogan Page, UK, 1997), a first impression is made in:

> One or two seconds. That's how long it takes for people important to you to arrive at their opinion of you as a person, or of your product or organisation. ... This is not merely a first impression – although it is that as well – but their whole opinion. Anything you say after those first seconds may help strengthen this opinion, or begin the long and difficult job to change it.

Author and psychologist Dr David Lewis goes even further in his book *The Secret Language of Success* (Bantam, UK, 1989):

> Research has shown that only seven per cent of the meaning of any conversation is contained in the words alone; the rest is communicated in body talk, in a whole vocabulary, grammar and syntax of posture, gesture, gaze and expression.

So, initial bonding with your audience is critical. If you fail to convey warmth, enthusiasm and confidence in those opening seconds, you'll certainly find it difficult to do so later on. And what easier vehicle than your greeting? You don't need a script, props, gimmicks or visual aids – just you and your energy. Walk up to that platform looking as if you want to be there. If, on the scale of 1–10, your natural energy level is 5, then up it to 7. Fill your lungs with air and *smile*.

Don't be in a hurry to start. Let your audience take a good look at you. Only then and without any reference to your notes, look them confidently in the eye, smile and begin. For example:

> Good morning, everyone. As our Chairman said, I'm Alex Tennant and I'm Director of Sales and Marketing. And I'm flattered to have been invited to share my thoughts with you.

This deceptively simply sentence has already sent some important signals to your audience:

- The smile conveys warmth, enthusiasm and sincerity.
- Use of the collective pronoun 'everyone' begins the all-important 'bonding' process.
- The touch of humility suggested in the word 'flattered' will go down well. Audiences can spot arrogance or lack of interest even before a speaker has opened his mouth.
- It never does any harm to identify yourself – even though you will almost certainly have been introduced. It reinforces ownership of your space.

So far, so good. They like what they see. What next? I make no apologies for repeating that the most important parts of a speech are the beginning and the end. Even an audience with dedicated self-interest won't listen in rapt attention to everything you say. You can rely on concentration at the beginning and the end, but you should make generous allowances for lapses of attention in between – all the more reason to make the opening and closing as compelling as possible. Some people refer to it as the 'grab and drive' technique: grab the audience's attention at the start, and drive home your message at the end. Scientifically, it's known as the laws of primacy and recency (see Anne Nicholls, *How To Master Public Speaking* (How To Books, UK, 1991)), and the print media lives by that philosophy.

As already outlined, there are many ways to sustain attention:

The personal pronoun

What audiences want to feel is your personal commitment. They don't like speakers who hide behind the corporate 'we', neither do they want to be spoken down to. But they do want to feel involved and they do enjoy being flattered. Using the personal pronoun is a simple and effective way of achieving these aims. For instance:

> Now I know most of you in this room today will remember the challenge we faced this time last year. ...

Examples

You can never have too many examples in a speech. When I'm training someone to deal with the media, one of the key requirements that I try to instil in them is the need for colourful, relevant examples. In the first unrehearsed interview with a trainee, examples are as rare as a puddle in the desert:

Reporter: And how would you assess your company's performance in the last year?

Interviewee: Oh, I'd say we're all very pleased. The Annual Report says it all really.

Not only has that answer not taken us very far, but the interviewer will have to keep up the pressure to elicit more information. How much more interesting if the interviewee had said:

Interviewee: You only have to read the first page of our

Chairman's statement in the Annual Report to know that we are all very pleased with our progress this year. We have increased our turnover by 6 per cent, our operating profit by 3.5 per cent, and our dividend will be 12 pence per share for the year.

As I said to Jim Bowls who, as you probably know, has worked with us for over twenty years, that dividend has been worth waiting for, and is evidence of our confidence in the future.

In 20 seconds, that reply, as well as sounding confident, contained some useful information that would reinforce the overall message of success:

- simple statistics – 6%, 3.5%
- promise of reward – 12 pence dividend
- personal reference to member of staff – conveying human face of the company.

The same principles must apply when scripting a presentation. If your intention is to impress your audience with the amount of money you are investing, by all means give them the financial data, but paint a picture as well:

So, what will all this investment actually mean to our customers? Whenever anyone walks into one of our refurbished pubs, wherever they are in the UK, the first thing they'll see is a real wooden floor. The artefacts will be real antiques. Real ale will be on sale. And as for the Yorkshire puddings, I challenge anyone to find bigger served in any pub. But most important of all, it's our guests who are important, and our staff know that.

The overall effect of this example is one of confidence, pride and enthusiasm. The illustration in this extract is simple and easy to remember. The repetition of the word 'real' reinforces the key message of quality, and the reference to the size of the Yorkshire puddings introduces a little humour.

Anecdotes

An anecdote mustn't be confused with an example. Few of us can resist a good story; not suprising, therefore, that they are so valuable as part of a presentation. They can act as an intellectual breather for both you and the audience: a buffer between key messages; a graphic and entertaining way of reinforcing a point; a means of changing mood or pace.

A word of caution. Don't save an anecdote until the end of a presentation. If you do, you will have difficulty in changing the pace and bringing your speech to an effective close.

Quotations

A quotation must be appropriate. If in doubt, leave it out. Unless it fits, a quotation will jar not only with you, but with your audience as well. I usually spend far too much time combing through numerous anthologies, ending up not using anything. They are, however, great fun to read and can often stimulate ideas for your speech.

Statistics

A simple way of getting attention is the use of the shock tactic of an arresting statistic. If you can relate it directly to your audience, so much the better:

> By the time I have finished this presentation, four people in the United Kingdom will have died from smoking-related diseases. Put it another way: if only one of those four had been able to kick the habit, the NHS would have been saved thousands of pounds in medical care.

If you are going to use a statistic in your introduction, resist the temptation to make it over-complicated. Remember, less is more.

Humour

I am a keen advocate of humour, simply because it's a wonderful relaxant for everyone. Furthermore, the creation of such an environment of goodwill will give you an additional shot of confidence. The use of humour at the beginning of a presentation can be a useful ice-breaker. Jokes, as I have already said in Chapter 5, can have the same effect, but must be embarked upon wisely. Don't be afraid to use humour throughout your talk, but sensibly. Most business presentations have a serious message, but humour can help to sugar the pill and get the message across.

For humour to work, it must be apposite, subtle and fast. If you can make direct reference to your audience, so much the better. Stuart Turner, in his admirable book *The Public Speaker's Companion* (Thorsons Business Series, UK, 1988), provides over 1,000 suggestions. I have selected a few of his (and also one of mine) as scene-setters.

> For those of you who have had a long day, I've booked an alarm call for the end of my speech.

> Look at it this way. I am the only thing that stands between you and a rum punch (Sarah Dickinson).

> No one is exempt from talking nonsense; the misfortune is to do it solemnly.

> If the speech goes well, I'll be invited back next year. If it goes very well, I won't have to eat the meal.

> At least that introduction was better than the last time, when my host asked me 'Are you ready to speak now, or shall we let them enjoy themselves a bit longer?'

> I asked your secretary how many men would be present, how many women, and how old you'd be. In market research terms, I asked if you were broken down by age and sex. He said he thought most of you are.

Humorous quotations are always well received as well:

> A bore is a man who, when you ask him how he is, tells you. (Bert Leston Taylor)

An expert is one who knows more and more about less and less. (Nicholas Murry Butler)

Statistics are like a bikini. What they reveal is suggestive; but what they conceal is vital. (Aaron Levenstein)

The minute you read something you can't understand, you can almost be sure it was drawn up by a lawyer. (Will Rogers)

Half the money I spend on advertising is wasted, and the trouble is I don't know which half. (Viscount Leverhulme/Ogilvy, *Confessions of an Advertising Man*, 1963).

You can bring added value to your humour if you can tailor it to your audience. Stuart Turner again:

He owes a lot to (the association). He owes a lot to Nat West/ Barclays, too.

They say 'see Naples and die'. When you see ... (town to be ribbed), it feels as if you already have.

Repetition

Despite the fact that we are all taught that repetition is to be avoided at all costs, in presentations the reverse is true. Remember, one of the fundamental differences between you and your audience is that you know where you are going and it doesn't. The only way to make sure a point sinks in is to repeat it.

Politicians are masters of the art, particularly in the use of the repetitive shopping list:

We will bring down inflation.
We will maintain employment levels.
We will remain loyal to our European allies.

Repetition of a single word can also be effective. The late UK Prime Minister Sir Athony Eden, during a television broadcast to the nation explaining why he was sending troops to Suez, used the technique well:

> All my life I have been a man of *peace*, working for *peace*, striving for *peace*, negotiating for *peace*.

A more familiar example of the technique is found in Abraham Lincoln's Gettysberg Address of 1863:

> ... this nation under God shall have a new birth of freedom ...
> The government of *the people* by *the people*, for *the people*, shall not perish from this earth.

Promises

Audiences come to listen to you for a variety of reasons. Whether their attendance is voluntary or compulsory, they will react in favourable unison if you make a promise early on in your introduction and then deliver it. For example, in my initial introduction to a media training seminar, I always promise the delegates that, if they stay the course, they will leave knowing how the media function and how to work with them. The promise is mutually useful. Trainees have an incentive to work hard during the course and I know that I will have their full co-operation.

Be wary, however, of overselling. Audiences are more and more outspoken these days and are likely, if you fail to deliver, to let their feelings be known.

Challenges

Group challenges are a good way of involving the audience and work well because no one is singled out for either praise or criticism, yet everyone can respond individually. Consider this example:

> I have only one message to all of you here today – by this time next year, we will *all* be reporting double-digit growth. That's my challenge to you all – double-digit growth.

Rhetorical questions

A rhetorical question is one that is asked not to elicit an answer but to produce effect, and is a useful device to use if you need to change tack, wake up your audience, or alter the mood.

Sometimes, the question can be deliberately provocative. Say, the subject of the presentation is about staff motivation. Instead of going straight into your 'menu', you ask the following question:

> How many of you in this room think that our Directors are paid
> too much? No, don't answer that. I raise the question, partly in
> jest, but partly because it gives me an opportunity to talk about
> bonuses.

If you do introduce rhetorical questions, always be ready for the one wag in the audience who *will* answer. Don't be put off by the interruption. Turn it to your advantage and engage in a brief humorous exchange. The rest of the audience will love it.

Audience involvement

'If you give audiences a chance, they'll do half your acting for you,' said Katharine Hepburn. Barry Humphries, the Australian comedian, in the guise of the suburban housewife, Dame Edna Everage, is merciless when he involves an audience. No hairstyle, outfit or piece of jewellery, if it's in his line of sight, is safe. To my amazement, the picked-upon seem to enjoy his attention as much as the rest of the audience.

Unless you are confident of being able to pull off a Dame Edna impersonation or something similar, you must never embarrass an audience by putting an individual on the spot. Stick to that rule and only seek group response. Asking for a show of hands often works well: 'How many of you in this room have ever had to face a hostile journalist?' It's a benign question that won't embarrass anyone and, whatever the response, will give you something to react to.

Another effective tactic is to appear to hand over the entire proceedings to the audience. Invite them to introduce themselves or ask a specific question of their neighbour. I draw the line at the American habit of encouraging physical contact, but there's no doubt that audience inhibitions are quickly broken down this way.

There's little difference between adults and the young when it comes to audiences. Both like to be given little treats. Handing out objects, the use of which isn't clear, is guaranteed to keep your audience clearly focused at the beginning of your speech.

If you know someone in the room, mentioning their name can by association create a sense of warmth in the audience.

> I see Peter Levy is with us this afternoon. I don't know whether to take that as a compliment, Peter. After all, you were at my last presentation. Didn't I say *anything* that made sense?

An extension of audience involvement is a pre-arranged question-and-answer interlude. Have a word beforehand with a colleague who you know is going to be in the audience. Ask her if you and she can have a brief public exchange at some point during your presentation:

> Jo Clark, I know you've had similar experiences when it comes to dealing with a fluctuating cash flow. How did you get around the problem?

There's nothing to stop you involving your audience at various times during your talk. It's a useful way to change the pace or wake people up.

Good use of visual aids

This topic keeps cropping up, which suggests how important it is.

If you're using illustrative material during an introduction, you must guard against showing something that will detract from your vital early bonding with the audience. For example, a video can often be an effective communication tool, but show it before you've established your identity and personality and I think you will have to work doubly hard to reassert yourself. A slide of your company's logo, on the other hand, is a non-intrusive and effective way of using a visual aid at the beginning of a presentation. I've also seen the use of a deliberately misleading picture as a way of grabbing audience attention.

Imagine the scene. A group of middle management has been requested to attend a presentation on the technology that went into making a new product. The entertainment potential is likely to be low. What a jolt to their expectations as they are greeted, not by a slide of the company logo, but an idyllic tropical scene. Up steps the Director of Technology:

> Good morning everyone. You thought you were coming to a briefing about the technology behind our new products. You're right – you are. That idyllic scene behind me was simply to make sure I had your attention right from the start.

There are very few people who can hold an audience without some kind of visual support. There are also very few people who can use such support effectively. Don't let your ineptitude with visual aids undermine the strength of your presentation. The next chapter will ensure that this does not happen.

Props

Like humour, a prop, if its appropriate, can be an effective way of breaking the ice with an audience.

The BBC Media Correspondent, Nick Higham, began a talk in 1997 by showing his audience a tiny piece of equipment on which he could not only record sound interviews digitally but edit them as well. In his other hand he held a large intimidating microphone. In times of such sophisticated technology, he went on to explain, the need for so large a recording instrument was redundant but it served as a useful prop to shore up his credibility. Big microphone; big assignment; important reporter. The audience relished this piece of insider information and the laughter that Nick's use of them provoked relaxed us all.

Shared props can be another way of breaking the ice. Give each member of the audience paper and pencil, balloon, dice – anything you like – teasing them with the promise of use at some point during the presentation.

➡ ENHANCING THE STRUCTURE

You should now pay a little more attention to enhancing the structure of your speech. In theory you've got through the greeting and delivered a strong introduction, and the feelings of panic should have subsided. You have engaged your audience by your sheer energy. You have grabbed their attention by employing one or more of the techniques already described. You have given them a clear idea of the overall subject matter of your presentation (the menu) and have settled them down by running through any necessary housekeeping points. The audience will instinctively appreciate that you are ready to begin on the main body of the speech.

The additional elements of structure to consider now are:

- bridging
- summarising
- concluding.

Bridging

Unlike a reader, a live audience doesn't have the benefit of signposts such as chapter headings, bold text, different fonts, paragraphs, indentations, punctuations or the white space surrounding the text – all of them clear indicators for the reader of change of pace, subject matter, priority etc. An audience has only your voice and your body language to help them through your speech. Verbal bridges are essential to take the listener easily from one point to another. Here are some examples:

In the last five minutes, I've taken you very briefly through the history of our company. *Now we come to the moment you've all been waiting for* (bridge) – our plans for the new millennium.

That story, courtesy of my local cricket club, was really *a scene-setter for the crux of my presentation today* (bridge) – why new business has to be the lifeblood of our organisation.

I promised to give you three reasons why I am confident we can achieve our marketing goal. We've already talked about two of them. *I'll now deal with the third* (bridge) and, in my opinion, the most important.

Summarising

Only an arrogant speaker fails to acknowledge an audience's 'nod-off' factor. However riveting you think your performance, people's attention will and does wander. Cast your mind back to when you were last in an audience: what was said half-way through? You will be hard pressed to remember.

It can happen to a presenter, too. I remember I was interviewing a spokesperson from a vinyl flooring company, in the days when I presented an afternoon consumer radio programme. We got off to a fairly predictable start, my guest responding to a not unreasonable question about the precise constituents of this type of flooring. I managed a supplementary question about how vinyl compared with other types of flooring, an enquiry which set him off on a litany of explanation. His jargon-infused response bored me, and no doubt the listeners – so much so that I wandered off into a reverie of food preparation for the evening meal. I had been so lost in domestic planning that I failed to realise that not only had he finished speaking but I hadn't registered a word he had said. It was only luck that my next question was appropriate!

You can help an audience through such lapses of attention by neatly summarising each of your main points:

> That deals with the visionary aspect of the future of this company. But, I know you are all quite rightly thinking, 'What is the use of vision if we don't have the resources to implement it?' This is the question I now intend to address.

The most helpful summary of all is the one that comes towards the end of the presentation. It should clearly and concisely recap on the main subject, leading naturally to the conclusion and sign-off:

> So, that's my game plan.
> Let me recap.
> From the time I joined GIC as New Business Director, I have been able to identify its unique qualities. I am clear that what we already have in place will help us begin to make a much more serious commitment to generating new business – but we need to do much, much, more. I am absolutely determined to fight, not only for myself but for everyone else in this room this

morning, for technical and intellectual support to make sure we can achieve Richard's goals, which, in case you missed them first time around are:

- to make GIC's advertising the best-known brand on the block;
- to develop – through teamwork – a consistently high standard of innovation and creativity; and
- to become a world leader in communication.

Concluding

Just as the final summary is an opportunity to herd the mental stragglers into your pen, so your conclusion is your last-gasp chance to make sure that they remember the key messages, if not the detail. Conclusions must be as arresting as beginnings. So often, usually because of a combination of fatigue and relief that the end is in sight, a speaker will undo all the good of his presentation simply by tailing off in a feeble whimper.

The conclusion must be bold and challenging. Leave them something to respond to:

We only have *one* course of action – we go forward, we don't look back.

I leave you with a challenge. We meet here in six months' time to report a 10% increase in turnover.

Although you want to end on a high note, you must make it absolutely clear when your speech is over. Some practised speakers finish on such a dramatic high that the simple act of tidying their papers will signal the end, to be followed by spontaneous applause. You can't rely on that, and it is safer to be more prosaic. Perhaps:

Ladies and gentlemen, thank you for listening to me this afternoon. That is the end of my formal presentation. I would be delighted to take questions.

Or

Ladies and gentlemen, thank you for listening to me this afternoon. That ends the formal part of today's meeting. I am looking forward to meeting you all later.

➡ **WHAT NEXT?**

Next, the chapter that I've been promising: visual aids and how to use them.

Chapter 7
Visual and other aids

Visual aids are different from prompts. Visual aids help your audience understand what you are saying; prompts help *you* deliver your speech. Microphones make sure everyone can hear you.

The visual aids that you might use are:

- white laminated board
- flipchart
- overhead projector
- slides
- computer-generated graphics
- audio or video clips
- hand-outs.

Your prompts could be:

- full text
- printout of overhead or slides
- cue cards
- autocue.

Your microphone could be:

- radio neck mike
- hand-held radio mike

- fixed mike
- hand-held mike

Let us look at all these in turn.

➡ VISUAL AIDS

I have a reputation for being savagely critical about the way
people misuse visual aids. I watch grown adults struggle to keep
their composure in presentation training sessions as I challenge
them to throw away their security blankets and talk to their
audience without visual aids. Such a 'cold turkey' approach
doesn't win me many friends, but it certainly makes the point
about the need to use visual aids wisely.

Unlike some, I am not totally against their use, but for them
to be effective, you should follow the simple rules given in
Checklist 7.1. Visual aids can come in various formats, as listed
above. I now comment on each of them.

Checklist 7.1   Rules for using visual aids

- Visuals are there for the benefit of your audience, not you.
- Think of them as headlines.
- An audience should never have to read a slide or overhead.
- KISS – keep it simple, stupid.
- Rehearse, rehearse, rehearse.
- Know your text well enough to be able to deliver the speech
  without the visual aids.

White laminated boards

White laminated boards are usually A1 size, consisting of a hard
white laminated and framed surface supported by a free-standing
easel. The surface can be written on and wiped clean so long as
special marker pens are used. Write boldly and clearly.

If you are presenting to a small group and want to encourage a degree of interactivity, they can be quite useful. I have a personal aversion to them as they are only one generation removed from the school blackboard and, as a result, create a rather institutional atmosphere.

Flipchart

A flipchart is usually the same size (A1) as a white board. Its advantage over a white board is that a pad of paper is attached to the frame, which allows greater visual variety. It is useful in a small 'brainstorming' group, when a facilitator needs to record ideas quickly.

Don't use a flipchart for meetings of more than twenty people. Try to avoid turning your back to your audience and, as with a white board, write in bold legible letters. There's an unkind joke about former American President Gerald Ford not being able to think and chew gum at the same time. Make sure, if you are going to use either of these visual aids that you can write or draw *and* talk at the same time.

Overhead projector

An overhead image is created by placing a piece of transparent acetate onto a light box. Once switched on, an enlarged image will be projected onto whatever surface you choose (a screen, a blank wall etc). The advantage of using overheads is that they can either be prepared beforehand or, as they can also be written on, used spontaneously. As with white boards, you need special pens. If you have the dexterity, an element of suspense can also be created by only revealing part of the sheet at a time. If you are going to use them, remember the vital points in Checklist 7.2.

Checklist 7.2   **Rules for using an overhead projector**

- *Never* reproduce the text of your speech.
- Try to get a variety of prints (fonts) and use upper and lower case and underline.
- Acetates are difficult to handle as they tend to stick together,

and will accentuate your nervousness as you try to prise them apart. Framing each one (in cardboard etc) will avoid these problems.

- Remember to clean the projector's reflector glass before you begin.

- Switch off the projector if there are long pauses between each image.

- However insecure you might feel, stand away from the projector. If you don't, the bright light will obscure your face.

- Make sure the projected image is in focus.

As with any visual aid, you have got to be able to use an overhead fluently. It must come across to your audience as an integral part of the presentation, not an apologetic add-on.

Slides

If you're going to use slides, it's as well to have them made professionally. Apply some simple rules to this use too, as set out in Checklist 7.3.

Checklist 7.3 **Rules for using slides**

- Don't use pale backgrounds: white text on dark works best.

- Make sure the text or diagram is big enough to be seen from the back of the room.

- Don't overcrowd the slide.

- *Never* reproduce your speech on slide.

- Make sure the carousel is the right way up.

- If the carousel is operated by a technician, make sure your cues are clear.

- Make sure the slides are in focus.

- Take a spare bulb with you (check the make).

- *Check and re-check*.

- *Practise*.

Computer-generated graphics

More and more people are using lap-top computers to prepare and display visual aids. 'Powerpoint' is the software generally used on IBM-compatible machines, and either 'Director' or 'Inscriber' on the Apple Macintosh. Once you've mastered the technology, there are many advantages to using images created in this way:

- easily and cheaply produced
- sophisticated
- colour
- movement – wipes/dissolves
- quickly changed
- compact
- immediate printout.

The image can be projected from the computer either onto a screen or a TV monitor. Whichever you choose, make sure that either your computer has a built-in composite video output or that the venue is able to provide a VGA-to-composite converter. If they can't, you should be able to buy one from a computer dealer.

The problem with using computer-generated graphics is your ability to both programme and operate the computer. As anyone who has ever tried knows, the computer mouse is a sensitive creature that doesn't respond well to clumsy handling. Just as you spend time rehearsing your speech, do make sure all your visuals are in order and that you are comfortable using the computer. If a technician is available, you might feel more secure putting him in charge. If you do, make sure that you stick to the cues in your script. This will reduce the risk of any surprises.

I was at a presentation recently given by a sales director to his marketing team. The speech was energetic and motivational and his computer-generated slides were effective. Beaming with confidence, he nonchalantly clicked his mouse, presumably to exit the programme. Imagine his surprise, and ours, when the message 'Good luck darling, sock it to them' came up on the screen. Administrative lapses aside, we were all curious to know who was the author of such a caring thought.

Audio or video clips

Audio and video clips can add value to a presentation, so long as they are well produced and relevant. The trap that most people fall into is to make them too long. If you're in any doubt about duration, use your own attention span as a yardstick. Remember, anything longer than a minute will tend to slow down the overall presentation.

If you do go for either audio or video clips make sure they are 'cued' up beforehand and that, if the playback machine is being operated by a technician, you have told her the *precise* cue words so that she knows when to activate the equipment and when to switch it off. Once agreed, you must not deviate from your cue words. In addition, ensure that everyone in the room can hear and see. Above all, *rehearse*.

Handouts

Few of us have grown out of the childhood habit of hoping for a present when we leave a party. It is quite a good idea to pander to this absurdity if you can. A copy of your speech and a printout of your slides is usually well received, as are free pens, notepads or product samples. But don't hand anything out until after you have finished speaking. A lecture I recently went to invited us to leave our names and addresses if we wanted to receive a complete set of notes. A clever marketing ploy, as it gave the organisation a useful addition to their database and a second chance to reach their audience.

➡ PROMPTS

To watch someone make a presentation without once having to look at notes is very impressive, but to do so requires a great deal of experience and confidence. You shouldn't feel inadequate because you need prompts – most people do. The aim is to find the middle ground between total dependency and apparent improvisation.

Full text

There are still a great number of people who only feel comfortable presenting if they have the full text in front of them. It doesn't matter to your audience, so long as your dependency doesn't prevent you from communicating with them. You must *never read a speech*. Instead, you must appear to use it as a prompt, so that you can maintain eye contact with your audience.

It will help if you print your text in 'camera' style. Write the speech on the right hand side, at least 1½-line spacing, and instructions on the left. Print your instructions in a different typeface from the text, and use highlighters to mark major changes – for example, when you are moving from the menu to your first main point. Some people even include instructions to 'pause, smile or look up; if you think it will help, put them in (see Appendix C). If you know your hands are likely to shake, get the pages mounted on card. At least that way they will be easier to pick up should you drop them.

Printout of overheads or slides

On the whole, this is never a very satisfactory prompt, simply because slides and overheads have been created for your audience and therefore won't contain the right information for you. Not only will you not give of your best if you try to present using only overheads or slides, but your audience will quickly recognise what you're up to and won't be impressed. They don't like lazy speakers.

Cue cards

Cue cards sized 4″ × 3″ (10 cm × 7.5 cm) are discreet, compact, silent, easy to handle and quickly reassembled if dropped. Some people attach them to a metal ring. Never write out your entire speech on them; doing so simply defeats the object. Work instead from the outline you used when writing your speech. See Chapter 9 for how to use your cue cards effectively. Whatever you write on your cue cards, always remember that the information is a *prompt*, not the full text. There are several ways of prioritising points:

- using upper and lower case
- differently sized and shaped fonts
- symbols
- colours – yellow and orange highlighters work well on cue cards

Autocue

Most people realise that presenters and newsreaders on television are not blessed with photographic memories but are reading from autocue – a small TV monitor placed just below the camera on which the presenter's script silently appears. Operated by a technician, the flow of the printed words follows the speed of the presenter's delivery. A similar system has been evolved for platform speakers. Known unofficially as a 'sincerity screen', a small glass panel is placed on a slim stand in front of the speaker. Reflected on to this is the text, again controlled by an operator who will follow the speaker's speed. Leading politicians often opt for two panels – one either side of them – so that they can enhance the appearance of spontaneity by appearing to talk to all their audience, not just those straight ahead of them.

Now that most autocue scripts are produced by computer, it is possible to build textural variety into them. For instance, you might be able to highlight certain words, or change the font for emphasis. Most systems can now produce words in both upper and lower case and some can print symbols. If you are going to use an autocue, always check which system will be used.

The secret to using autocue convincingly is to remember that *you* control the speed of the flow of words on the screen. Slow down, and the flow of words will also slacken; and vice versa. To make your delivery as natural as possible, you should build spontaneity opportunities into your script. For instance, don't write in every single word, but do signal stage instructions such as 'pause', 'new point', 'summary'. Don't laboriously write out an entire anecdote. Simply remind yourself and your operator by keying in 'anecdote- – hot air balloon adventure'. Make sure that you return to your official text as marked on the autocue. Your operator is not a mind-reader.

You mustn't be a slave to your autocue. Reading from the glass screen is no better, from the audience's point of view, than reading from a piece of paper. And bring your cue cards with you, just in case the equipment breaks down – this will give you added confidence and also the appearance of spontaneous thought. If you can imagine that a friend is behind the screen on which your words appear, you will sound much warmer.

As with all things, unfamiliarity is the enemy. It is not difficult to use an autocue, but it takes practice. It goes back, yet again, to knowing your speech. If you have the speech structure firmly in your head, you won't have to rely so heavily on the autocue, which will allow you to maintain eye contact with all of your audience. Autocue is a *prompt*, not a text.

➡ MICROPHONES

There are four types of microphone that you might be offered for voice amplification:

- radio neck mike
- hand-held radio mike
- fixed mike
- hand-held mike.

Radio neck mike

This is the system I would recommend that you ask for if you are going to need a microphone for your presentation. It consists of a small transmitter, not much bigger than a cigarette packet, with a slim wire leading from it to a very small microphone, which is pinned either to a collar or tie. The transmitter is usually fixed at waist height.

The advantage of this type of microphone is that, once an engineer has adjusted your voice level, you can forget all about it. You can also move freely around the platform. One or two minor things to remember:

- Make sure you have a pocket or belt to which to fix the transmitter.
- Attach the mike upside down to avoid the amplification of 'popping' on hard consonants.
- Make sure the small aerial on the transmitter doesn't get caught. It will crackle if it does.
- Turn off the microphone when going to the loo.
- Take spare batteries with you – most radio mikes use size PP3.

Hand-held radio mike

These microphones are popular with stage performers. Although they have no transmitter or wires, they do have to be held, which could present difficulties if you're not used to them. If you do use one, hold it a few inches below your chin so that it does not obscure your face. These microphones can be sensitive so, to avoid the risk of microphone 'howl' or 'popping' on hard consonants, don't hold them too close to your mouth.

Fixed mike

A fixed microphone is usually attached to the front of the lectern. Some of them are adjustable, in which case make sure that it stands about level with your mouth. Most fixed mikes are now omni-directional, which will give you a little flexibility of movement but not much. To ensure that your audience doesn't 'lose' you, don't stand more than two feet away from either side of it. As with a hand-held mike, be careful not to get too close to it because microphones exaggerate sounds. You should avoid the following:

- noisy jewellery
- chest-thumping (known as Tarzanning)
- wearing materials that rustle

Hand-held mike

The only difference between a hand-held mike and a hand-held radio mike is the addition of an electrical cable. To prevent cable crackle, don't let it rub against your clothing and don't fiddle with it. Wind the cable round your wrist a couple of times to take the strain off the connection between the mike and the wire. One final tip: be careful, when you're moving about, to keep the cable behind you so that you don't trip over it.

➡ WHAT NEXT?

Preparation of your presentation material and ancillary items should now be complete. Your speech has a subject, a structure and verbal and visual illustration. Now is the time to get your nerves under control.

Chapter 8
Controlling your nerves

'Everybody has the capacity for an open, expressive, connected voice. It is only tension blocking the route. We can all benefit from learning the actor's skill of breathing freely, however nervous we are.'

(Susan Henry, voice coach)

The late Lord Olivier said he was often physically sick before going on stage, and anyone who has had to give a presentation will recognise why. However much time they have devoted to preparation and rehearsal, most people will admit to still feeling 'sick with nerves' just before they start to speak.

The symptoms are depressingly familiar. Thumping heart, trembling legs, sweating palms and pallid complexion. Some people complain of their mouth becoming as dry as an African desert or their intestines gurgling like early Victorian plumbing. Without exception, everyone reports a sense of panic at loss of breath control. All these unpleasant sensations are side-effects of the body reacting to stress. When we are frightened, the body automatically goes into 'flight or fight' mode.

This response is brought about by the action of the hormone adrenalin, produced by the adrenal glands situated above each kidney. It acts on the autonomic nervous system, which controls the function of the heart, blood vessels and digestive system. When the body is facing a physical emergency (and it may well perceive as one the moment before 'presentational lift-off'), the autonomic nervous system increases the heart rate and diverts blood from the skin and digestive organs to the muscles, getting you ready for action. This redistribution of blood to the skeletal muscles from the internal organs can also produce the uncomfortable symptoms already mentioned, as well as draining colour from the skin and making the fingers ice cold. These natural responses to stress would be useful if you were about to slay Goliath or flee a burning house, but not very helpful if you've no one to fight and no reason to flee.

A state of stress increases your blood sugar level as glycogen, the carbohydrate stored in the liver, is converted into glucose and released into the blood, giving you an energy boost. The problem, biologically, is that this will only be a temporary state, and the body will automatically release insulin to lower the level. The stress hormones also result in unpleasant side-effects such as excessive sweating and thirst – not helpful for a polished performance.

So what control can a quaking presenter bring to bear over his or her body in a state of heightened arousal? Put at its simplest, we must try and control our breathing and see-sawing blood sugar levels, hope to slow down our metabolic rate and somehow trick the brain into believing that the crisis is over.

There are three aspects of this trickery:

- learning to breathe
- learning to eat
- rehearsing

and each is explored in greater detail below.

➡ LEARNING TO BREATHE

As Susan Henry said, everybody has the capacity for an open, expressive, connected voice; it is only tension that blocks the route. We can learn the actor's skill of relaxing enough to channel our nerves so that we can breathe and speak freely, even when we are very nervous.

Anybody who has spoken in public starts with the same intention. They want to reach their audience and they want their voice to convey what they feel and think. All babies are born knowing exactly how to do this. They convey their needs vocally without any inhibition. If they want food, they cry – sometimes very loudly. As adults this openness has been lost through social conditioning, so that we become inhibited in the way we communicate. When we have to speak publicly, that inhibition is magnified, so afraid are we of being judged. Not surprisingly, we can become daunted by, and sometimes physically frightened of, the prospect of the performance.

If you are not aware of this state, says Susan, and try to deny that the tension exists, it becomes very difficult to do anything about it. The more you try, the more effort you put into it, but if that effort is being sent to the wrong places, it only makes the problem worse. Once you realise that *nerves can help* you and be your ally, you can even begin to enjoy the performance. Try to think of tension as blocked energy. Release the tension block and you release an injection of creative energy into your system.

Undirected stress can affect you vocally in many ways:

- Cause you to speak too quickly, obscuring your message.
- Induce shallow breathing, which will prohibit rhythmic delivery.
- Flatten and dull the tone, preventing you from making use of inflection.
- Raise the pitch, making you sound even more nervous than you probably are.
- Stiffen your jaw, thereby affecting the articulatory areas – tongue, teeth and palate – and producing gabbled or stumbling delivery.
- Dry out the mouth, making it difficult to articulate.

One of the first things we notice when we're nervous is a change in the rhythm of our breathing. We seem compelled to take quick, shallow breaths, rather than deep, regular ones. Our shoulders and chest tense, which in turn restricts the pharynx (the muscles inside the neck) and the larynx (the voice box), making it more difficult for air to pass freely through the passageways, and reducing control over our voice. Try speaking with your mouth hardly open; then try speaking with it as open and as wide as is comfortable. The difference in the sound you are able to produce will be marked.

For the breath to move freely and deeply, the body needs to be aligned and free of tension. The following exercises can heighten awareness of the potential areas of tension in the body and help develop the right supporting muscles for full breath support. Susan Henry suggests a number of exercises to help you release negative tensions and learn how to build on your natural voice.

Exercises to release tension

Exercise 8.1 Relaxing the body

Lie down on the floor and raise the knees. Release the weight of the body into the ground. Tense and release each area of the body individually. Flex the feet up towards the knees and release, letting a breath go out with the release. Tighten the legs and buttocks and release, letting a breath go. Press the back into the ground and release, and then the neck and shoulders, tightening and releasing and letting the breath out with a sigh. Think of the back lengthening and the shoulders spreading broadly across the floor.

Exercise 8.2 'Centring' the breath

Let go of all thoughts, except the one that instructs 'I do not need to hold on'. Give your jaw a quick message and let it drop open as naturally as possible. Let the breath drop gently in and out of the body on a sigh-like *haaaah*. To enhance your awareness of this relaxed breathing pattern, place one hand just below your navel and feel the rise in the stomach as the breath fills deep into the body and then how the stomach lowers as the breath drops out.

This is how the body works when the breath is supported naturally from the diaphragm, a convex muscle that separates the chest and abdomen and plays an essential part in breathing. The breath is 'centred' rather than high in the chest.

Exercises to develop the voice

Exercise 8.3 Connecting the voice

Breathe out on a *sssss* sound for a few breaths, then on a *zzzzzz*. Feel the vibration of the voice hitting the teeth and the top of the tongue on the *zzzzzz* and carry this forward onto the lips, so that you are humming *mmmmmmmmm*.

Exercise 8.4 Building your breath capacity

Once you have established a relaxed breathing pattern, you can build on it by counting the amount of time you hold the breath sounds *sss*, *zzz* and *mmm*, and by gradually increasing the time. Start by holding *sss* for a count of five, build to ten and fifteen and so on, but keep checking for body tension as you do so. If some tension should creep in somewhere – shoulders, neck and back are vulnerable tension areas – tense and release that area of the body and go back to building the breath count more gradually. Over time, this will strengthen the muscles and enable you to support longer breaths.

Exercise 8.5 Building your range

Go back to the centred breath on a gentle whispered *haaaaaaah* sound and let a trickle of sound sweep along it in a sigh-like curve going from high to low pitch. As with the breath, work only with your natural capacity to start with. Do not reach for notes that are too high or low or feel uncomfortable. Keep doing this, adding a little more voice (volume) to the breath each time.

Now catch whatever is the highest note you reached, and speak a piece of text all on that one note. Just for the fun of it, try these instructions for setting up a printer:

> The printer is equipped with an 8-bit parallel interface port for connection with IBM-PCs and compatibles. The interface port accepts only a Centronics-type parallel interface cable; if you need help selecting the right cable, consult your dealer. The IBM-PC family and compatibles send data to the parallel interface port by default when the power is turned on, so no further set-up is necessary.

Do the same with the lowest note you reached. Speak the text alternating word by word between high and low. Speak it again really over the top using as much silly exaggerated range as you can, as if you were a melodramatic Shakespearean actor. These exercises should reveal to you how many notes you have accessible to you when you are relaxed and just playing with the voice. Now speak the text normally and enjoy the freedom of being able to use range to actually make sense of the text.

Exercise 8.6 Building your volume

The volume of the voice depends on resonance. Resonance could be described as the vibration and amplification of the voice in a resonating area. Most of the human resonating areas lie in the skull and mask of the face. If you hum and put your hands on your lips, you will feel some vibrations. The amazing thing about vibrations is that they grow. They cause more vibrations around them in the face and eventually in the airwaves around the face and body. And this, broadly speaking, is how the voice carries through the air. To build your vocal volume, therefore, you want to build as many vibrations as possible.

Hum to yourself. Any tune will do. Think of the sound buzzing forward onto the back of the lips and then spreading around into the front of the face, into the forehead, the nose and then onto the chest.

Practise speaking a piece of text that has a lot of humming-like *mmmmmmm* sounds in it. Really linger on the *mmmm* and *nnnn* sounds as if you are speaking the piece in slow motion: 'The moon beams seem to stream across the dreamy scene.'

Exercise 8.7 Building your articulation muscles

Yawn and stretch. Yawn again, thinking of making the yawn round, so it really stretches the soft palate. Exercise the back of the tongue with *kkkk* and *dddd* sounds with the tip of the tongue, and *wwww*, *vvvv* sounds with the lips. With all these sounds, start slowly and precisely and speed up as the muscles warm up.

Massage the face and jaw and chew gently, imagining a small piece of gum that slowly gets bigger and bigger.

Try speaking the following tongue-twister slowly and then gradually speed up:

She stood upon the balcony
Inexplicably mimmicking him hiccuping
And amicably welcoming him in.

If you are preparing to speak from a speech written by someone else, practise beforehand speaking the text in an exaggerated manner or in slow motion. This will help you to define any problem words and will programme the articulation muscles for the job in hand.

People take in words much more slowly than we can speak them. If you go too fast, your audience will still be thinking about what you have just said, while you will already have moved onto your next point. If this happens, they will not hear what you say next. Give them time to think and yourself time to breathe. Remember that your pauses will always seem shorter to an audience than they will to you.

Exercise 8.8 Building authority with pace

Practise your text, taking a centred breath between each punctuation mark and speaking each clause using the whole breath, even 'it's' and 'so'. This will really slow you down. Tape yourself speaking at this pace. You may be surprised at how some of it sounds perfectly 'normal'.

Remember that each exercise is part of a warm-up routine, which should be practised regularly to have effect. Practice will ensure that the voice is there when needed, and will create the enjoyment of vocal freedom.

➡ LEARNING TO EAT

'What we eat prior to giving a performance will dramatically affect how we feel,' says nutrition consultant Alli Godbold. 'You'll give your best performance when your blood sugar is balanced, and the secret to obtaining the right level lies in eating the correct ratio of carbohydrates and protein at the right time.'

Carbohydrates eaten on their own release too much sugar into the blood, making you feel hyperactive, a condition that then triggers the release of insulin to lower the sugar level. Protein leads to the release of glucagen, which pushes the sugar level back up. In other words, a vicious circle is created. To achieve the right balance, Alli Godbold recommends a ratio of two parts carbohydrate to one part protein to produce an ideal blood-sugar level.

How do we know if our blood-sugar levels are not as they should be? If your levels are persistently imbalanced, you will experience the following symptoms:

- waking up feeling sluggish.
- feeling you need more than eight hours of sleep.
- being drowsy at certain times of the day.
- an excessive thirst and sweating.
- frequent hunger pangs – a craving for sweet foods and starchy carbohydrates, as well as stimulants such as tea, coffee and chocolate.

What to drink

In order to give an already nervous presenter a fighting chance, *what* should we drink and *when?* In this regard, Alli Godbold is not an advocate of a 'quick fix' through high energy drinks simply because the sugar is released almost instantly into the blood stream – too quickly for the average person's needs. She also urges that all drinks that contain stimulants, such as coffee, tea, diet cola or other colas, should be avoided because these exacerbate symptoms of stress, such as heart palpitations. Not that I can imagine anyone wanting to do so, but drinking milk just before a performance is also not recommended, if only because it can create a lot of mucous in the throat, which you'll want to clear. Throat-clearing is not an elegant sound and is best avoided.

Some people swear by a nip of brandy or whisky to give them courage. Although alcohol does act as a depressant, it doesn't discriminate about which areas to depress; so, inevitably, you won't be in as much control of your performance as you should be. Have as much as you like once it's over, but *not* if the press are around – that performance afterglow, coupled with an alcoholically loosened tongue, makes you an ideal media target. The most useful lubricant is non-carbonated water; herbal tea, especially mint, is also refreshing and aids digestion.

Always insist on an ample supply of water during a presentation. As I have said, your throat *will* dry and it will need to be lubricated if you are not going to suffer from a terrifying throat tickle.

What to eat

To repeat Alli's nutritional mantra: the body appears to respond best to a diet of two parts carbohydrate to one part protein. It certainly doesn't need extra sugar – two teaspoons of sugar are approximately equivalent to what is optimally contained in our eight pints of blood. Refined carbohydrates are also less beneficial than unrefined ones because they rapidly deplete energy levels. Foods that should be avoided are shown in Checklist 8.1.

Checklist 8.1 **Foods to avoid before making a presentation**

white bread/pastry	chocolate
white pasta	crisps
white rice	

On the other hand, certain carbohydrates are definitely on the 'good for blood-sugar level' menu, and the choices for protein are even more straightforward. See Checklist 8.2 for details.

Checklist 8.2 **Foods to eat before making a presentation**

Carbohydrates	Proteins
whole grains, including brown rice and quinoa (which comes from the Andes in South America and contains a good level of vegetarian protein – Godbold says it cooks like cous-cous and makes a delicious salad)	white meat
pulses – lentils, beans and chickpeas – combine carbohydrates and protein and can be eaten in full measure	fish – including smoked salmon (fresh salmon is even better)
whole-grain brown bread/ whole-wheat pasta	soya products, eggs nuts and seeds selected dairy foods.

To make a presenter's culinary decision-making process as simple as possible, Alli Godbold recommends that you choose from the following light snacks to eat about *one* hour before 'curtain up':

- smoked salmon sandwich on whole-grain bread
- breast of chicken salad with rye bread
- quinoa salad with brown bread

At all costs, avoid the temptation of the quick sugar snack. It will, as with the high-energy drinks, give your blood-sugar levels a sudden boost, which will then quickly drop, setting up the unpleasant see-saw effect.

If, despite following all this advice, your nerves still feel jangly, you can always take the homeopathic route and try Argentum Nitrate – look for 'Arg. Nit.' on the bottle. Film directors swear by it, as do actors, as it seems to provide the antidote to panic, especially in the run-up to a performance. Sold in tablet form, follow the instructions and take a dose the night before a performance or presentation, and again a couple of hours before the event. Following the principles of homeopathy by giving the body a little of what it is suffering from, the symptoms are alleviated. So, tight shoulders and clenched jaws relax, and a sense of calm prevails that, in turn, frees the mind to concentrate.

There is also, says UK's TV presenter Kay Avila, the famous standby of television 'green rooms', the place where guests are required to wait, in petrified limbo, before their turn on screen. This standby is known as Bachs' Rescue Remedy: a few drops under the tongue or in a glass of water has calmed many a terrified guest, and a few presenters too. It's a cocktail using flowers like Star of Bethlehem, clematis and rock rose, which, according to its fans, takes the heat out of any shock, trauma or performance, without impeding the brain cells.

➡ **REHEARSAL**

In the next chapter, there is no turning back. It's time for the performance, the moment to capitalise on all that preparation. But not before you have made time to rehearse. *Never underestimate the importance of rehearsal. The more you practise, the less anxious you will feel.* There are two stages of rehearsal, the private and the public.

Now that you have the final draft of your presentation and have virtually settled on your visual material, you should do a complete, timed run-through in private. The timing element is essential, as it will immediately indicate whether more editorial work needs to be done. If the speech is short by, say, two minutes, don't immediately rush to fill it with extra words. Think about your presentation. Did you rush it? Did you leave any room for pauses? If it's too long, on the other hand, then you *must* trim the text.

Once confident that it is running to time, find a willing colleague to watch your second run-through. You will not only get some valuable feedback about the content, but even an audience of one will make you perform. If you can video your presentation, even better – you will learn so much from playing it back. Did you swallow your words? Were your gestures appropriate? Why didn't you smile? Did you look at the audience enough? A video playback will answer all these questions even more than a colleague. Unfortunately, video exaggerates imperfections, so don't lose heart: learn from the experience and rehearse the speech again. You are guaranteed to improve. When you are satisfied with the whole presentation, don't rehearse it again until you get to the venue, assuming that there will be time for you to do so.

To keep your nerves in check, as soon as you arrive inspect the following:

- lighting
- height of lectern and microphone
- visual aid equipment
- sound system
- glass of water

Lighting

Unless you are taking part in a sophisticated light show, you have a right to determine how brightly you should be lit. Don't go overboard, however, on asserting your authority. So long as you can read your cue cards or text, and the audience can see you and your visual aids, it shouldn't matter what level the lighting is. What you must avoid is being taken by surprise.

Height of lectern and microphone

Most lecterns are adjustable. During your rehearsal, make sure that you find your correct height and that you can easily adjust it if the previous speaker had it at a different one. The first public speech I made taught me this valuable lesson. I hadn't allowed enough time to check the venue, let alone rehearse. So I had only myself to blame when I walked up to the lectern to discover that not only was it not adjustable but it concealed most of my face. I remember bravely stepping out from behind it, to discover that I'd left my notes on the top. Unshielded and noteless, I gabbled through my presentation and finished about ten minutes ahead of schedule. It is not an experience I have ever repeated.

Some lecterns have a fixed microphone. It will usually be attached to a flexible metal wire, which can be easily bent to suit the speaker. Make sure during the rehearsal that you know the exact level to set it at. For the most effective sound, the microphone should be level with your mouth. If you're going to use a radio mike, practise attaching the transmitter to your person and fixing the microphone as described earlier. The 'on/off' switch is generally very small, so you should make sure you know how to operate that as well.

Visual aid equipment

A professional conference centre should always find time for you to do an audio and visual check. Take the opportunity to ask if there is time to run through your presentation as well. If there isn't, *insist* that you check your visuals and audio and video clips. Once you've rehearsed with them, make sure that *everything* is rewound to the beginning. I once attended a meeting of people interested in the audio book market. With a great flourish, one of the speakers invited us to listen to a selection of extracts from some of his best-selling audio tapes. Not only were we kept in silent suspense as the operator fumbled to cue the tape but when he did eventually find the place, the wrong one was played.

Sound system

Not only check that *your* microphone needs are catered for, but also anyone else who might be involved in your presentation. For instance, if you're going to involve your audience, or someone else on the platform, be sure that the organisers know so that they can accommodate you.

Glass of water

Liquid refreshment for a speaker is often forgotten. If you've the slightest suspicion that it won't be provided, make a point of asking for it.

➡ ONE FINAL CHECK

Once satisfied that the support systems are in place, check that you have brought everything with you that you need:

- copy of speech
- props (if any)
- copy of programme
- business cards
- handouts
- spare tights (if appropriate)

Perhaps most important of all, allow plenty of time to get to the venue. While you're waiting for your turn, discreetly work on some of the relaxation exercises outlined earlier. Read through your speech notes and familiarise yourself with the names of other speakers. And, finally, remember, as I once saw on a door of a TV dressing room: 'This too will pass.'

➡ WHAT NEXT?

You can't put it off any longer. It's time for your performance.

Chapter 9
The performance

'This above all – to thine own self be true.'

(Polonius, from *Hamlet* by W. Shakespeare)

The moment has come. A roomful of people are waiting to hear you. You have dutifully followed the guidelines of this book, so you have a strong subject. You know that what you are going to say will be coherent and has been crafted to take into account your audience's lack of knowledge and expectations. You know the profile of your audience, your visual aids are appropriate, you have anticipated the kind of questions you are likely to be asked, and you have checked the venue.

Why do you still feel so vulnerable and nervous? As I explained in Chapter 8 about controlling your nerves, it's simply your adrenalin kicking in which you have learned to embrace, not fight. It is now that not only must you believe in yourself that you *can* deliver your presentation, but that you can deliver it with energy, flair and passion. You are ready to *perform*.

Don't try to be someone you are not. If you are known for your quiet speaking voice, don't try and emulate the style of the Rev. Jesse Jackson; similarly, if you have a reputation for being a bit of an office wag, don't adopt a professorial style. If you try to be anything other than yourself, you won't feel comfortable and your performance will be unconvincing.

Some people are natural performers. My parents tell me that when I was ten, people used to flock to our local church to hear me read the lesson. I may not be a natural performer any longer, but I certainly enjoy entertaining people – *if I'm fully prepared*. An effective way to get into the right frame of mind is to imagine yourself performing in a play. You've learnt the lines, which you may have written yourself, had some control over the set and lighting, and chosen your costume. You are ready.

The problem most people face is that although they know they are sufficiently prepared, they are lacking the belief in themselves that will enable them to perform. Actors can press the performance starter-button any time. I've mentioned already how you can help yourself by calibrating your natural performance level on a scale of one to ten. If you're honest, you'll probably put it at about five. For a platform performance, this is not good enough; don't be fearful of appearing to go 'over the top'.

Can you think of anyone whose 'over-performance' grates? TV personalities Peter Snow and botanist David Bellamy are both colourful, energetic communicators; they both wave their arms about and Bellamy sounds as if he's speaking through a mouthful of Brussels sprouts. We might be amused by their foibles, but I doubt many of us switch off when they're on. If you are going to get through to an audience, you have got to be a little bit larger than life. Upping your energy levels a couple of notches will certainly help.

Another incentive is the giddy anticipation of applause. If you perform well, people will show their appreciation. One of the most remarkable, unexpected responses to a speech Britain has ever witnessed came at the end of Earl Spencer's tribute to his late sister, Diana, Princess of Wales, at her Westminster Abbey funeral service on 6 September 1997. The promises he made and the challenges he set in that address were so forceful that the crowd outside broke into waves of spontaneous applause, which filtered into the Abbey and moved the congregation to break with funereal tradition and join in.

Before looking at the many things you can do to improve your performance, some mannerisms to avoid are listed in Checklist 9.1.

Checklist 9.1   Mannerisms to avoid

- Looking over the top of half glasses appears arrogant and supercilious.
- Adopting a supplicant manner to promote your cause.

- Waving arms and hands around as if struggling to put up washing on a windy day.
- Constantly clearing your throat.
- 'Erring' and 'umming'.
- Never looking at the audience.
- Dropping names.
- Keeping hands in pockets.
- Talking to overheads.
- Ending with a 'whimper' not a 'bang' (apologies to T.S. Eliot).

You have been warned. Now it's time to get to work on *you*. We shall look at ways of controlling your body, voice and props.

➡ CONTROLLING YOUR BODY

There are four aspect to controlling your body, each described in more detail below. These are:

- posture
- gestures
- movement
- eye contact

Posture

The question I am most often asked is whether to stand or sit when giving a presentation. There are no rules, but I would recommend that you stand whenever you can: it shows confidence and gives you control over your audience. The possible exceptions would be if you were giving a one-to-one presentation, a small, informal seminar or lecture, a TV or radio interview, or were chairing a panel during a question session. The trickiest decision as to whether to sit or stand is when you're presenting, usually with overheads, to a small group, a board or managerial team seated round a table. One thing is certain, you *must* present at the *head* of the table.

Posture reflects what you think about yourself. Averted eyes, lowered chin, hunched shoulders, splayed feet and restless hands send out signals of low self-esteem. If you're going to present to an audience, you have got to literally 'walk tall'. When you step onto the platform, your back must be straight, your shoulders back and head held high, your arms relaxed at your sides and your face showing eager anticipation. If you intend to stand for your presentation, avoid welding yourself to your lectern. How many times have you sat in an audience and laughed silently at a speaker clutching the sides of the lectern like a life raft?

All of us have different ways of standing. The most important thing is to be natural and comfortable. If you have always stood with the weight on your left side, then continue to do so. But take a look in a mirror just to make sure that your leaning to one side doesn't make you look unbalanced or sloppy. The best way to stand is with your legs a body-width apart, with hands and arms held loosely at your sides. At least try *starting* that way.

The same principles of comfort apply if you're giving your presentation sitting down. Try and make sure you have a chair that is the right height and doesn't swivel. If your feet can't touch the ground, your balance will be affected. You'll instinctively feel at a disadvantage and that sense of unease will affect your performance. The swivel chair was designed by a sadist. The anthropologist Desmond Morris has a fascinating theory as to what we're really doing when we swivel from side to side. He suggests that we are unconsciously reacting to the fight-or-flight instinct: we want to stay and give our talk, but we'd also like to escape. The struggle between the two imperatives results in constant swivelling, which displays our anxiety and at the same time distracts the audience.

The ideal sitting position is to get your bottom as far back in the seat as possible, and then lean the trunk of your body slightly forward. By doing so, you are giving your audience a silent, but effective signal that you want to talk to them.

Clothing is affected by how you sit. A jacket will ride up above your collar unless you remember to pull it well down as you take your seat. In the same way, skirts deserve attention.

There is much discussion about whether or not to cross the legs. On the whole, I'd recommend doing so: it adds interesting line to the body and will prevent nervous foot-tapping. The one seated position that both men and women must avoid is the 'Widow Twankey' posture. This is where the person slumps in the chair with legs wide apart. Not only is it extremely ungainly, but it rivets the eye on the genital area. There is also the 'half-way house' posture to consider. It's a pose favoured by academics – perching on the corner of a desk, half sitting, half standing. So long as you want to create a mood of informality, it is certainly an effective choice, supporting your body but still leaving you free to move, turn and gesture.

If you are standing and sitting correctly, you will find it easier to control your limbs. Under stress, our body, with its various appendages, assumes its own control. As Sigmund Freud once said:

> He that has eyes to see and ears to hear may convince himself
> that no mortal can keep a secret. If his lips are silent, he chatters
> with his fingertips; betrayal oozes out of him at every pore.

I remember working on a speech with a man who swayed so violently from side to side during his presentation, that we both felt sea-sick. If he had stood as I suggest, this problem would not have arisen. Just as distracting is the person who sways backwards and forwards. There is a greater danger of this happening if you put your hands behind your back – a posture I would not recommend, not least because you can't gesture.

Feet seem to give people trouble. As if in response to an internal musical instruction, a presenter's foot (it's usually one, not both) will begin tapping. The problem with this kind of activity is that, although your audience will be watching with increasing fascination – will the other foot join in, will you suddenly break into a dance routine? – you will be totally unaware of what you're doing and the effect it is having on the audience, and they won't be listening to what you are saying. A way of preventing these kinds of nervous reflexes is to shift your posture from time to time. Uncontrollable knee jiggling is another sign of nerves. Again, if you know that you have a tendency to do this, keep subtly shifting your posture.

Gestures

All of us display unconscious physical gestures, which, when we are nervous, are exaggerated and detract from the effectiveness of our performance. It would probably surprise a balding man to see that he constantly stroked his forehead as if coaxing his hair back. He might not realise, too, that he bites his lower lip, fiddles with his ear lobes or jingles coins in his pocket. These are known as 'displacement activities' and should, if possible, be minimised. The more confident you are, however, about your presentation, the less likely you will be to undermine your performance with such unconscious mannerisms.

Conscious gestures, on the other hand, are an essential element of a presentation. They tend to fall into three categories:

- positive
- signposting and emphasising
- challenging

Positive gestures

The most positive gesture of all is, of course, your smile. If you manage to do nothing else with your body during your presentation, but you remember to smile as you walk on to the platform, you will have gone some way to bonding with your audience. People are always concerned that smiling indicates lack of seriousness. This isn't true. A wide grin can be misleading, but an animated face with a suggestion of a smile will always be appropriate at the beginning of a speech.

British Prime Minister Tony Blair's wide, generous smile is instinctive, and serves him well when he's meeting people. But in his electoral campaign portrait, unlike previous studied photographs, he wasn't smiling; and these days, during important speeches, he smiles less often. He has learnt to control the grin to good effect.

As well as smiling at the start of your presentation, you mustn't forget that it's a useful communication tool throughout. If you've said something humorous, reinforce it with a smile. Remember, however, that there is a big difference between a smile and a laugh.

You won't offend your audience if you smile after a witty observation, but they won't appreciate it if you laugh as well. In contrast, though, if someone in the audience says something that amuses you, do laugh.

The main value of gestures during a presentation is to unite you with your audience. But, just as you have to vary the pitch and pace of your voice, so you have to vary the size of your gestures: *The more important the point, the bigger the gesture.*

Supposing you want to make a big impact right from the start, the surest way to do this is to appear to physically embrace your audience:

> It is a great honour to stand here in front of so many colleagues and be given the opportunity to share my ideas.

This statement can be reinforced by the speaker stretching his arms wide apart, with his palms open towards the audience.

Arm movement is also a useful gesture to use when illustrating the breadth of a topic – the slight variation being such that you can build on it:

> We shall not leave a county of this country untouched. We shall start in the West (*gesture with right arm*), the East (*gesture with left arm*), the North and the South – as I said, the whole of the United Kingdom (*stretch out both arms*). And this is where I need your help (*both arms outstretched with palms open towards the audience*).

There will inevitably be times during your speech when you want to be positive but less emphatic. Try using only one hand to gesture with:

> It's not really something we should concern ourselves with right now – it's more a question of you and me (*gestures back and forth to audience with the lower half of the right arm and open hand*) keeping an eye on what's going on.

So long as it doesn't look affected, cupping your chin in your hand can be an interesting way of positively suggesting the need for further consideration:

> I think everyone here will agree we've got a tricky decision to

make (*either cups chin in hand or supports chin lightly with thumb and index finger*). Do we want to run the risk of letting our competitors know what we're up to? ...

Pointing at oneself sends out a very different message from the one conveyed by pointing at the audience. It works well when reinforcing a rhetorical question:

Want to know what I (*points at self*) think?

or when you want to make sure that the audience knows who is in charge:

This is my (*points at self*) responsibility and I'm not afraid to take that responsibility. If you've got any thoughts or doubts, I'm (*points at self*) the one to talk to.

Signposting and emphasising

Hands and fingers are valuable when you need to signpost. For instance, when you're running through a list of points, use the fingers on one hand to count them.

Some emphasise a point with their hands. They do this either by slicing the air at the precise moment they want to emphasise a particular word or, as with the counting technique, re-emphasise each point by ticking it off on an up-held hand.

Challenging gestures

There was a memorable World War I poster depicting Lord Kitchener looking straight ahead and pointing a challenging index finger. The message beneath was simply 'YOUR COUNTRY NEEDS YOU'. If you really want to challenge your audience, then pointing at them will leave them in no doubt as to your intentions. But it's a gesture that must be thought about before you use it:

I think you're a bunch of feeble, indecisive parasites (*points angrily at audience*).

That type of remark and finger pointing won't be well received – even if you might believe what you're saying. On the other hand:

I can't begin this journey without you (*points finger*).

It's *your* project, *your* idea (*continue to point finger*). I'm simply
here to help you realise it.'

The raised fist is a gloriously confident and challenging gesture.
It tends to be used by trimphant sportsmen, aspiring military
leaders and sometimes victorious politicians. If it fits the tone of
your speech, it can serve as a very useful 'call to arms' at the end.

One final word about geatures: they can enhance a performance,
but only if they are controlled and confident. When you start
practising, they will probably feel forced and unnatural, but they
might, if you persist, become part of your individual style.
Nevertheless, if they don't, don't force them.

Movement

How much should you move around on the stage? Before we
entered the recent technological revolution, speakers didn't have
much choice. The only way their voice could be heard was via a
static microphone permanently fixed to a lectern. This would
occasionally be attached to a piece of flexible wire that allowed a
degree of height adjustment but, if you moved even a few inches
away, you would become inaudible.

With the advent of radio microphones, the speaker can move
freely, confident that she will be heard, so long as she's sure it's
switched on. Movement will bring yet another dimension to your
presentation and help the all-important bonding process, but you
should be wary of it becoming habitual. We've all silently tittered
at the lecturér who paces back and forth, always turning at
precisely the tenth step.

Prime Minister Tony Blair broke with tradition in the run-up to
the 1997 UK general election when he abandoned the lectern and
autocue and talked to his audience from the edge of the stage. His
actions might have sent Peter Mandelson into paroxysms of
anxiety, but they were well received by the crowd.

One final point about movement. Although you are now free to
move as you please, it is dangerous to get separated from your cue
cards. So, don't leave the lectern to walk towards the audience if
there is any risk you will forget what you are going to say.

Eye contact

'When the eyes say one thing and the tongue another, a practised man relies on the language of the first' (Emerson, 1860). Take a few minutes out and watch a TV comedian and see how he uses his eyes to exaggerate a point. None of us needs to go to such extremes, but it should quickly convince you of the power of eye contact.

I once trained someone for a presentation who told me that, because the lights prevented him from seeing his audience, he didn't think it mattered where he looked. How wrong he was. Even if you can't see your audience, *they can see you*, and if you fail to make eye contact with them, they will quickly lose interest in you and your presentation, which is why speakers who read their presentations instead of only referring in passing to their notes find it so difficult to make any impact. You must establish *immediate* eye contact, for in doing so you will take control of the proceedings. Don't just set your line of sight on an individual in the middle of the front row; look at people to your left, then to the middle, then to the right, and then repeat the process.

➡ CONTROLLING YOUR VOICE

The first time you heard your voice recorded, you were no doubt disappointed when told that that was exactly how you sounded. Apart from the actors who are paid for their dark chocolate voices, no one is ever comfortable with how they sound.

However, unless the way you speak makes it difficult for people to understand what you're saying, it doesn't matter what you sound like. Regional accents are attractive, as are slight verbal imperfections such as an inability to pronounce the letter 'r ' or 's' properly.

Once you've overcome your natural inhibitions about how you sound, you can begin to concentrate on getting the very best out of your voice. This book is not about elocution or speech therapy; however, it will help you make the most of a valuable presentational tool. Variety in your voice can be achieved by:

- volume
- pause
- pitch
- pace.

Volume

As has already been stated by voice coach Susan Henry, we can all make much more of our voices if we know how to. We've also discussed how nerves can strangle the voice, raising its pitch and reducing its volume. Henry points out the importance of resonance, and suggests the exercises given in Exercise 8.6 of Chapter 8 to help you build volume:

> The volume of the voice depends on resonance. Try saying it, and you'll immediately get the picture. Resonance is the vibration and amplification of the voice in particular parts of the body. Most of the human resonating areas lie in the skull and mask of the face. If you hum and put your hands on your lips, you will feel some vibrations. Rather like the increasing circles created by throwing a pebble in a pond, vibrations grow. They cause more vibrations around them in the face and eventually in the airwaves around the face and body. Broadly speaking, this is how the voice carries through the air to your listeners. To build your vocal volume, therefore, you want to build as many vibrations as possible.

It is much easier to fill a room vocally during a performance if you have already had the experience of hearing your own voice filling that space. If you get a chance to see the space where you will be making your presentation, do the following exercises in the room.

Exercise 9.1 Filling the room

Hold your hand about six inches in front of your face, breathe in and allow a stream of voice to move to your hand on a *zzzz*. Do the same holding your hand further away. Look at a spot on the nearest wall to your breath, and let the voice travel to that spot. Do the same to the wall furthest from you.

Take in the whole room in a semicircle, breathing in as you look, and let the voice move into that semicircle. If you are relaxed in your body and breathing from the centre, you will find that you *automatically* take in the right amount of breath to fill the space.

Just as it isn't sensible to fix your eye contact on a single person in the audience, nor is it wise to deliver your entire speech at full volume. If you do, your audience won't be able to determine which aspects are important and which are less so, and will probably leave with the uncomfortable sensation that they've been harangued.

Lowering the volume can be a very effective way of emphasising a point. It's the sudden change that alerts the audience to a change in priority. For example

> (*Normal volume*) So, that's what Scotland thinks about us here in England: they don't want us.
> (*Lowered volume*) Do we care?
> (*Normal volume*) Well, strictly between you and me, ...

Equally dramatic effect can be achieved by choosing wisely when to raise the volume. It is often appropriate in the final rallying-call of a speech.

Exercise 9.2 Increasing the volume

If you want to practise this technique, try speaking out loud the extract below from Shakespeare's *Henry V*, Act IV scene III – the speech just before the Battle of Agincourt:

> We few, we happy few, we band of brothers;
> For he to-day that sheds his blood with me
> Shall be my brother, be he ne'er so vile
> This day shall gentle his condition:
> And gentlemen in England now a-bed
> Shall think themselves accurs'd they were not here,
> And hold their manhoods cheap whiles any speaks
> That fought with us upon Saint Crispin's day.

Pause

There is an old Persian proverb that 'Speech is silver, silence is golden', and it is well worth remembering when you're giving a presentation. A pause, at the right moment, can make a dramatic impact on an audience. The trick is to know when to pause and for how long. Get it wrong in either respect, and the audience will begin to think you've lost your place. In principle a pause shouldn't last longer than three seconds. For example:

We will continue the search until every can of infected soup has been found [*pause*] and I mean every can.

Consider Winston Churchill's speech to the Canadian Parliament in 1941:

... and when I warned them that Britain would fight on alone, whatever they did, their Generals told their Prime Minister and his divided Cabinet: 'In three weeks England will have her neck wrung like a chicken [*long pause*].' Some chicken! [*long pause*] Some neck!

Pitch

You will only be able to control the pitch of your voice once you've managed to control your nerves, which in turn will be helped by learning to control your breathing. As a rule, the more slowly you speak, the lower in pitch your voice will sound; conversely, if you speed up, the lighter it will sound. Just as I am an advocate of varying the volume of the voice in a presentation, so I believe in the need to change the pitch. In Lady Thatcher's early speeches, her voice was high-pitched and unconvincing. Later speeches showed that she had learnt to change it – and so can you.

Intonation or modulation is an acquired skill, but it is useful to remember that a sentence that is finished on an *upward* inflection will denote unfinished business and a *downward* inflexion usually completes an idea. For instance:

I ask you all, is there not some way of resolving this issue (*upward inflection*)?

I believe what we are talking about here is integrity – integrity and courage. If we stick by those principles, we cannot fail. Ladies and gentlemen, thank you (*downward inflection*).

Pace

Nothing is more tedious for an audience than to have to listen to a speech delivered at precisely the same speed throughout. Varying the pace will alter the pitch of your voice and help emphasise important points. For instance, headings or subheadings, should always be delivered slowly, leaving plenty of silence ('white space') around them; similarly with summaries and conclusions. But you can speed up your delivery on less important parts of the speech, particularly when you're covering familiar ground.

➡ CONTROLLING YOUR PROMPTS AND PROPS

There are very few people who can give a speech without some kind of memory jogger. And, remember, even those who do will only have reached that stage of confidence because they have worked very hard on their preparation.

If you only feel safe with the full text in front of you, make sure that you type it up in the style of a TV autocue, a described in Chapter 7. Much better, however, if you have the confidence, is to use cue cards (see Chapter 7 for a description and Chapter 1 for an example of use). They are unobtrusive, easy to handle, compact and don't rustle. You should use them only as prompts, and never write out the whole speech. They can be annotated with symbols for the different sections of the speech, as described in Chapter 4. And remember that, even though securing them with a metal ring will keep them in the right order, it is sensible to number each one in case they inadvertently get shuffled!

➡ DRESS AND GROOMING

What you wear is a major contributing factor to the impression you make on other people. If you treat what you wear simply as a costume that suits a role you are about to play, you are unlikely to feel so self-conscious. In other words, dress to fit the part: if you're talking to members of a youth group, it's unlikely you would turn up in a formal suit; in contrast, if you've an important presentation to make at a board meeting, something formal would be more appropriate.

Unlike television, which can exaggerate the smallest detail, you won't generally be under such close scrutiny up on a platform, but you must avoid unnecessary distractions. An undulating hem line or unstitched trouser bottom can easily divert an audience's attention, as can the wearing of tennis-ball sized earrings or brightly buckled shoes.

Before deciding what to wear, find out what kind of event it is going to be. If it is an evening function, then you could be asked to wear 'black tie'; if it's daytime, then a lounge suit is the norm.

If your hosts invite you to dress informally, do so. I recently worked with the British entry for the Round the World Whitbread Race and was instructed to dress casually. Initially, I was resistant as I felt jeans and a sweatshirt lacked authority. I was wrong.

Checklist 9.2 gives some pointers to effective dress and grooming.

Checklist 9.2　Dress and grooming tips

- Always wear something you like and that others have complimented you on.

- Make sure your clothing isn't too tight, as this can restrict breathing.

- Shoes affect balance, so avoid anything too high or too tight.

- Don't buy something new the day before and don't go in for a radical change of style – you will feel self-conscious.

- Go for simple, unfussy lines. Tiered layers and flounces might look good on the dance floor, but they won't help your presentation.

- Women should always wear something that can be seen from the back of the room. Muted beige and browns tend to disappear into the furnishings. Similarly, men shouldn't be afraid of brightening up a business suit with a colourful tie and/ or top-pocket handkerchief.

- If you wear a digital watch, make sure that any beeping reminders are switched *off*.

- Women should make sure there are no runs in their tights – even the smallest one will spread as fast as a collapsing set of dominoes. Always have a spare pair with you.

- Men should be wary of the nasty hairy gap, the 'NHG factor', that can appear if your socks are too short and, when you are seated, expose an expanse of unattractive white, hairy flesh.

- Remember that your audience will probably be viewing you from the ankle up, so pay as much attention to shoes, hosiery and hem lines as you do to your hair.

- Hair should be tidy and clean and not obscure your face.

➡ LIQUID REFRESHMENT

To counteract a dry mouth, always make sure that you have something to drink to hand. Still water is the most refreshing, followed by tea. Avoid caffeine drinks such as coffee and colas, and above all *no alcohol*. Some people use a glass of water as a useful performance prop. The physical act of drinking creates a natural pause which can be used as a moment to allow a point to register or suggest a change in direction.

If you find yourself without something to drink and you feel your mouth drying, try gently biting the tip of your tongue or running it across the roof of your mouth. Both actions will make you salivate.

Unless you want to give the impression of the eternal student, don't walk onto the platform carrying a styrofoam cup.

➡ INADVERTENT MISTAKES

As I have already said, standing up in front of a group of people and delivering a speech is one of the most testing things anyone can do, mainly because of the fear of public ridicule. This anxiety is, of course, magnified by the knowledge that, almost inevitably, you will make a mistake. Mistakes don't matter so long as you have the confidence not to let them unhinge you when you make them. If you appear flustered and upset, your audience will lose confidence and stop concentrating.

The legendary American TV variety show host Ed Sullivan was famous for getting his words or facts wrong. He once referred to Irving Berlin as 'the late Irving Berlin'. Clarinetist Benny Goodman was introduced as a 'trumpeter' and off-camera Barbra Streisand became Barbra Streisland. He welcomed Dolores Gray as 'one of the fine singing stars of Broadway, now starving at the Alvin Theatre'. Singer Connie Francis remembers; 'You never knew what he was going to say. Once, at a dress rehearsal, after I sang "Mama", he said, "Come over here young lady and take a bow. Tell me, Connie, is your mother still dead?" (Nick Tosches, *Vanity Fair*, July 1997). Whatever his shortcomings, Ed Sullivan ruled the TV airwaves and hosted more than a thousand shows. He was not flustered by his mistakes.

The key to avoiding mistakes lies, of course, in preparation. If you can visualise the structure (greeting (—), menu (●), houskeeping (▲), main body of speech (▬), summary (■) and conclusion (✦)), you will always have something solid to return to, should you lose your place or make a mistake, and in that way you will avoid feeling mentally marooned. If you *do* get something wrong, and you think your audience may have spotted it, own up but don't be over-apologetic. For instance:

> You probably spotted just now that I referred to a 30 per cent increase in turnover. I wish! I should, of course, have said 13 per cent.

And what if you miss out a whole section? If it's not critical to the structure, ignore it, especially if you're not providing a printed text later. I remember interviewing the TV chatshow host, the late Russell Harty. At the end of a long and revealing conversation I admitted, off-air, to a momentary regret at not having asked him certain other questions. He tapped his large nose and said, 'Sarah, *they* don't know that.' Sound advice.

➡ AN AURA OF CALM SELF-CONFIDENCE

This chapter began by urging you to believe in yourself and your ability to perform, for if you don't, your presentation will never rise above the average. There are many things you can do to bolster your self-confidence.

TV presenter Kay Avila believes that tapping into past experiences that evoked a sense of well being can be helpful. She refers to this self-belief as surrounding oneself in a 'circle of confidence', a visualisation based on a system of 'anchoring' used in neuro-linguistic programming, NLP. Avila states:

> Remember a time when you felt really confident – maybe passing an exam or a driving test, or getting your first job – and recreate the feelings of confidence generated by that success. Watch how you feel and how you stand and log those positive feelings. Repeat this exercise at least four times using different situations, all of which evoke positive feelings. Draw an imaginary circle around you and enter it, again summoning feelings of confidence. Let them register and then step back outside the circle. Repeat a few times to ensure that you can easily access those positive feelings. Tell yourself that the only 'you' allowed inside that circle is the 'confident you' and that there is no room for your negative side. It is worth mastering the technique of 'anchoring' as it will enable you quickly to draw your past confident experiences into the present. You will know that, by simply stepping into the circle, you will be able to muster the confidence you need to make sure you give your best performance. Even the cynical who distrust mindgames know that everyone looks and sounds better once they get rid of negative thoughts.

Another broadcaster, Brenda Ellison, who spent several years working in the United States, helps interviewees or presenters overcome their nerves by introducing them to her 'tush push' technique; 'tush' being Jewish American for 'butt' or 'bottom'.

> This is basically a visualisation technique, which is a great confidence-booster and also helps the speaker to 'take his status', which is so important for audience first impressions.

Imagine that you have placed on your 'tush' a huge pair of warm, loving hands. They must be the hands of the person who loves and believes in you more than anybody else. There is no need to reveal their identity. Once those imagined hands are in place, your feelings of self-worth will increase. You'll no longer feel alone and, with your bottom tucked in, will find yourself 'standing tall'.

This exercise, carried out just before 'lift-off', will do wonders for your confidence and posture. It will also bring the beginnings of a warm smile. Out of a repertoire of nearly a hundred, this 'happy to be here' smile is difficult to reproduce under stress, so it must be practised. The wrong smile, particularly at the start of a presentation, will give the game away that you're not feeling too good about talking to this audience.

As well as recognising that heightened self-confidence will improve your performance, remember the importance of making a good first impression. There is no time for a warm-up when you're presenting; you must 'hit the ground running'. If your energy level is high, your performance level will be too.

Voice coach, Susan Henry, has some discreet pre-performance tension-reducing exercises, as given in Checklist 9.3. She also suggests that, before you begin speaking, you should take a moment to look around the room and take in your audience. You will instinctively take in the right amount of breath to carry the voice to them. She believes that an audience will respond positively to your self-imposed pause, understanding that you are taking time to think about what you are going to say.

Checklist 9.3   Tension-reducing exercises

- Massage your face, especially your jaw. Yawn and stretch (this will open out the throat).

- Mouth silently through your text to 'pre-programme' your muscles.

- Raise your shoulders to your ears very tightly, and then drop them with a sigh. Gently roll them backwards and forwards.

- Release the neck. Drop the head down onto the chest and sway it gently from side to side.

- Stand with your hand on your stomach and feel the breath movement drop deep into it. Focus on a spot on the wall opposite you. Let the breath stream out from the diaphragm in a steady flow to that spot on an *sssss* sound. Add some voice making it a *zzzzzz* sound. Bring the sound onto the lips in an *mmmmm* sound. Build up those vibrations and the solid sense of connection between your diaphragmatic breath support and your voice.

Even after a good start, some people suddenly experience a rush of stage fright half-way through their presentation. A few discreet body checks will help, as given in Checklist 9.4.

Checklist 9.4   On-the-spot body checks

- Are you standing correctly? If your feet are too close or too far apart, you won't be balancing the weight of your body evenly, which will make you tighten your stomach muscles to hold yourself up. This in turn will affect your breathing.

- Are you tilting over onto your toes or rocking back on your heels? If so, go back to basics and make sure that your feet are firmly grounded, about a body's-width apart.

- Is your body beginning to tense up? A few discreet tensing and relaxing exercises, as previously described, should help.

- Has your mouth dried? Remember how to use your tongue to help you salivate. Take a sip of water.

➡ WHAT NEXT?

Whether you adopt some of these techniques to help your presenting skills is up to you. What is absolutely central to the success of your presentation is that you deliver it with conviction, energy and enthusiasm. If you look as if you're enjoying it as well, you will have the audience eating out of your hand. Remember, they are on your side, they are *not* out to get you. As Robert H. Jackson, author of *Advocacy Before the Supreme Court: Suggestions for Effective Presentation* (1951) said,

'I always feel that there should be some comfort derived from any question from the bench. It is clear proof that the inquiring Justice is not asleep.'

In the next chapter, I look at how to answer questions and deal with interruptions.

Chapter 10
How to answer questions and deal with interruptions

Most speakers are wary of questions from the audience. It probably goes back to a schoolchild's fear of not being able to find the answer. I take a positive attitude, and view unrehearsed questions as a valuable opportunity to relate to an audience and promote interaction. However, unless you anticipate and stage-manage the questions, you could find your fears compounded.

➡ ANTICIPATE THE QUESTIONS

The most effective way to deal with questions is to be ready for anything. In a media interview, it is easy to anticipate the questions you will be asked because journalists tend to work with very few. Audiences are less predictable. They are not professional interviewers, and so their questions will often be irrelevant, unintelligible or repetitive. Also, unless you have had prior warning or recognise people in the audience who have asked questions before, you won't know who is going to raise their hand.

Although most people would sacrifice their lottery winnings rather than ask a question in public, there are certain recognisable types who need no second bidding. A breed to watch out for is the seasoned question-raiser. He will have a completely different agenda from yours. He will use the opportunity to ask a question as an excuse to air a point of view, often totally unrelated to your talk. He will plough on doggedly, until stopped. If the rest of the audience don't come to your aid by telling him to get on with it, *you* must: firmly but politely tell him to either ask his question or let someone else have a chance.

The other potentially tricky person to handle is the individual who uses the public arena to ask a controversial question only marginally related to your presentation. This is a technique much favoured by the media. Say the Secretary of State for Health accepts an invitation to open a nursing home in his local constituency. He uses the opportunity to reconfirm the Government's commitment to care of the elderly. A local journalist decides to question him, however, on the threatened closure of several local pre-school playgroups. Although not directly related to the speech, the question is valid and should be answered.

Many questioners, usually because of lack of experience, find it difficult to phrase their query succinctly or intelligibly. It is your job tactfully to interpret for them, just as it is your job to be able artfully to turn an irrelevant or repetitive question to your advantage.

You may, of course, be lucky, and only get asked questions that allow you to reinforce some of the key points you have made during your speech. Even if you don't, once you've mastered the technique of making the most of whatever is thrown at you, you will quickly be persuaded of the value of the exchange.

Just as you are in control of your presentation, you must be in control of your audience. In order to ensure that you are, you must listen very attentively to each question. If a questioner loses his way, help him out by interpreting the question and then answering it. If someone is getting carried away by the sound of his own voice, have the confidence to interrupt and urge brevity. If someone is hogging the floor, move on to someone else. Never forget, it's *your* occasion just as much as it is theirs.

If you take a positive attitude towards a question and answer period, the effort will be worthwhile. Invariably the interaction with your audience will help cement the relationship and give you a further opportunity to emphasise some of your key messages.

➡ **STAGE-MANAGING THE QUESTION TIME**

Having made the decision to invite questions, it's important to let the audience know at what point in the proceedings to ask them.

Unless you have a very disciplined time-keeper, it is not sensible to take questions during your speech. Your attempt to answer will inevitably throw you off-course and you will not reach the end in your allotted time.

If your text is divided into self-contained sections, questions at the end of each section could be appropriate but, again, be very strict with your time. Most people follow the tradition of taking questions at the end. If you want questions to be part of your presentation, you should allocate approximately 25 per cent of your time to them. For example, if you've been given a sixty minute slot, leave fifteen minutes for audience participation. Although you will have already let your audience know the procedure for questions during the early 'housekeeping' section of your speech, it is as well to remind them in a form such as:

> Ladies and gentlemen/colleagues/friends, that's the end of the formalities. I'd be delighted now to take questions. We've got about fifteen minutes. If you do want to ask me something, would you kindly raise your hand, wait for the microphone to be brought to you, give your name and where you come from, and then ask your question. I should warn you, I'm going to be very strict on supplementaries: one each, I'm afraid.

Every speaker's nightmare is the fear of there being *no* questions. We've all sat in a room and suffered on a speaker's behalf, as a deathly hush descends after his invitation. There are several reasons why people may appear reluctant to ask questions:

- a fear of making a fool of themselves.
- a fear of revealing lack of concentration, perhaps by raising a matter that's already been dealt with.
- *you've* covered everything, so there's nothing left to ask.

A way has to be found to get the ball rolling. This can be done by using some of the techniques given in Checklist 10.1. With any luck the flame of curiosity will have been lit by one of those ruses, and your only challenge will be to bring the session to a close on time. You must let your audience know when time is running out.

If you are acting as both chairperson and speaker, your final duty to your audience is to clearly indicate the end of the session.

> We've got time for two more questions ... yes, the lady over there and then you sir. Then we must end.

Checklist 10.1   **How to coax questions from an audience**

- Make sure there are a couple of people in the audience who have prearranged questions to ask.
- Get the host or chairman to ask you something.
- Ask the audience a question.
- Ask yourself a question: 'The question I'm most often asked is ... Let me take you back to what I said earlier. ...'
- Spontaneously select someone you know and challenge them to ask a question. This is a high-risk strategy and should only be tried by experienced presenters.
- Be visually alert and coax a tentative questioner with direct eye contact.

➡ INTERRUPTIONS

Audiences want you to do well but it is unrealistic to assume they will give your their undivided attention or listen in silent awe throughout. I still find it off-putting when I fail to hold an audience's attention, or, unintentionally, provoke interruption.

I once trained a small group of European chest physicians. They were all responding reasonably well to my entreaties, except for a large gentleman from one of the Benelux countries. I anticipated, by his lack of eye contact, that he'd probably be difficult, but I hadn't expected him arrogantly to open his mail during my introduction and then fall asleep. I ignored his bad manners and waited for sweet revenge during his simulated television interview, when I innocently asked whether he made a habit of falling asleep at work and, if so, couldn't this be rather alarming for his patients. He feigned incomprehension, but didn't convince.

Arrogant indifference, however tedious, is nevertheless easier to deal with than interruptions. As they are unexpected, they invariably break a speaker's flow, sometimes to the point of mental paralysis. If you possibly can, *ignore* interruptions unless they legitimately require a response. If someone urges you to speak up, then acknowledge the request and do so; if, on the other hand, someone rudely suggests you 'get on with it' or 'get a proper job', then remember your 'circle of confidence' and carry on. If you're feeling sufficiently confident and bullish, the audience will admire a quick verbal retort such as 'If the gentleman in the blue shirt would stop interrupting, I could get on with it.'

There is a legendary story of masterly control over an interruption that is purported to have taken place at a sales conference. An American, we'll call him Hank Schneider and give him the title of Vice President, was addressing his team. He was in full motivational flow, comparing the skill of closing a deal to that of landing a jumbo jet. Out of the corner of his eye, he noticed a side door opening. A woman, in a highly agitated state, marched to the front of the hall, turned, pointed to a man and a woman in the second row and shouted, 'That man is my husband and I want to know what he was doing with *that* woman last night.' With a degree of aplomb not usually associated with Americans, the speaker took a sip of water, waited for the commotion to subside and carried on as if nothing had happened. That's style.

Somebody deliberately 'walking out' of a presentation is the ultimate insult and can temporarily sabotage the concentration of both speaker and audience. Fortunately it doesn't happen often and if it does, ignore it.

➡ **WHAT NEXT?**

You've made your presentation and handled questions from the floor and word of your competence is beginning to spread. You are invited to talk to the media. The next chapter tells you what to do.

Chapter 11
How to be interviewed by the media

Giving a media interview, although different from presenting or dealing with questions from an audience, requires the same skills: the need to be prepared, and an ability to communicate effectively.

Once you acquire a reputation for being an able spokesperson, you mustn't be surprised if people start putting you forward to be interviewed. Don't be daunted by the prospect. As with public speaking, giving a media interview should be viewed as an inexpensive and persuasive way of getting your message across. And, so long as you've done your homework, and you know the rules, you will succeed.

A media interview, be it radio, press or television, is essentially a *game* – an important game, but a game nevertheless, and one in which each player wants to score points and win. People are often concerned by the use of combative words like 'winning' or 'losing'. They shouldn't be. The mental determination to 'win' as opposed to merely 'surviving' will dramatically sharpen your performance.

Always remember that it is through the interviewer that you get to *your* audience, while the interviewer uses you to fill *his* air time or column inches. There is no need to be coy about these mutual needs. The more co-operative and informative you are, the easier it will be, and the greater the likelihood of winning the game.

➡ THE JOURNALIST'S ROLE

Understanding a journalist's needs is the important first step towards a successful media interview. Is it surprising, when they seem to hold all the cards, that we are so fearful of the media? How many of the following descriptions would you recognise?

- They are assertive and opinionated.
- They are at ease with the environment and you are not.
- They make you think they can read your mind.
- They ask the questions, you provide the answers.
- They are only interested in bad news.
- They won't report you accurately.
- They are out to get you.

We look at each of these in turn.

They are assertive and opinionated

There are very few journalists who approach an interview with a completely open mind. Like you, they are subject to all kinds of influence: their own or their organisation's political attitude, their education, their personal experiences etc. Their approach to a story will always be coloured by this background and will invariably help form *their* 'angle' to each story. Unless you ask, few journalists will divulge the contents of that agenda beforehand. But you have every right to know.

It is certainly true that many journalists, especially those who work for the tabloid press or who cover politics, are assertive and aggressive. They want a reaction, and they think the way to get one is to push you to the limits. If you are in control, this tactic is less likely to work. Be wary of quietly spoken interviewers (who may still be opinionated), who quickly lull you into a sense of familiarity that lowers your defences.

They are at ease with the environment and you are not

We are all much more comfortable in a familiar setting, but it shouldn't matter where the interview takes place so long as you remember to concentrate your attention on the interviewer and not on any of the distractions around you.

They make you think they can read your mind

Interviewers can make you feel exposed and vulnerable by seeming to read your mind. They may ask, from their point of view, a straightforward question, which – only by chance – appears to you to disclose knowledge of information that you thought was confidential. This will disconcert you, but remember that you know more about your subject than they ever will and, if you have prepared for the interview, you will feel in control.

They ask the questions, you provide the answers

Your attitude towards an interviewer is key to taking control. You must treat a question always as an opportunity to get *your* point across. You are there to tell your story, not to endorse the journalist's. Unfortunately, politicians have so blatantly abused the protocol of interviews that they have undermined the value of this type of communication.

I'm often asked whether it's a useful tactic to turn the tables and ask the interviewer a question. Unless you are feeling *very* confident, this is a dangerous ploy. Even if they suspect it may not be so, interviewers like to think it's their show and they are the ones in control. Publicly challenging their assumed authority usually results in a stinging dressing-down:

> I hate to remind you, Mr Charles, but it is *my* job to ask the questions, and *yours* to answer. ...

It's very difficult to regain composure after that kind of exchange.

They are only interested in bad news

Let's face it, bad news is exciting – especially news of human catastrophe, for it undoubtedly sells newspapers and increases viewing figures. However, the majority of media output in fact comprises the reporting of non-sensational news.

It is importrant that companies and organisations understand this and foster the reality of media requirements by maintaining good contacts. Persistence will eventually pay off. If you have been regularly supplying your local paper with news about your company, even though nothing may yet have made the printed page, at least they will be aware of your existence. When they next need comment from a local industrialist, they could come to you rather than one of your competitors.

They won't report you accurately

Unless you put your points across clearly and succinctly, there is every chance that you won't be reported accurately. You will, all the same, blame the journalist although *you* will have contributed to the misreporting. What often happens, particularly in a print interview, is that because you have spoken too quickly, not communicated your idea simply or given the wrong signals through your body language, the journalist will rely instead on his *interpretation* of the conversation. It is up to you to make sure that he has registered what is important to *you*. If you are in any doubt, take control at the end of the interview and ask him to read back passages where you suspect misunderstandings may have arisen. Don't be afraid to repeat points. Often, the last thing on a journalist's mind is the first thing to appear in print.

A word of caution about mis-reporting. Some journalists justify attributing a quote to you on the grounds either that you failed to counter a supposition or that your body language appeared to endorse one. Here is an example.

Journalist: 'It must have been such a strain on your family during the merger talks. You were probably never at home and your children, let alone your wife, hardly saw you. Stronger men would have gone to the wall. How much did the whole exercise cost the company?'

The interviewee, understandably, is focused on the question rather than the preamble. Nonetheless, he is nodding in agreement to the journalist's descriptions concerning the effect on his family. Although risky, the journalist could attribute his own observations to the interviewee.

Article: 'It was such a strain on the family during the merger talks. I was never at home and my wife and children hardly ever saw me' said John Jones, Chief Executive of Hydrosalination Ltd in a recent interview.

John Jones was understandably angry when he saw the article and believed that he had been inaccurately reported, but it was his own fault.

Be wary of allowing a journalist to put words into your mouth. Don't, however, become over-sensitive about being reported out of context. Unless wrongly attributed remarks could damage the reputation of you or your company, let it go. A misquote in an article might wound your ego, but it will quickly be forgotten by everyone else.

They are out to get you

Journalists are fond of quoting Harry Truman's advice, 'If you can't stand the heat, get out of the kitchen' in defence of their sometimes maverick approach to news stories.

If you can avoid the unscrupulous media personnel, you will find that most journalists are *not* out to get you. They want a story that's colourful, informative and lively, which will please readers, viewers and editors. If you can deliver your points with a dash of confidence as well, you'll find yourself entered in their electronic organisers and asked back. If, on the other hand, you come across as weak and dithering, you are quite likely to trigger their 'killer instinct' and they *will* get you.

➡ STYLES OF INTERVIEW

Interviews fall into roughly three categories, each of which is described briefly below.

- Information seeking
- Expert opinion
- Confrontational

Information seeking

Most interviews fall into this category. You are the source of the reporter's information, the reporter merely a conduit for your ideas. Although they may be elaborately dressed up, the reporter only has six basic questions: who, what, when, why, where and how?

Expert opinion

There are rich pickings available if you can persuade a newspaper journalist or a television or radio producer that you have specialist knowledge. The reporter knows there is a need merely to press your 'on' switch and you'll do the rest. Not only will you be unlikely to get hostile questions – the interviewer wouldn't have the gall to give you a hard time because you are giving him such an easy one – but you will be holding centre stage and will have numerous opportunities to promote your company. The local media especially welcome expert opinions, and it is worth cultivating key contacts to make sure that, when a situation arises, you are the one they phone for comment.

Confrontational

As its style suggests, this is potentially the most hazardous type of interview. Film reporter Roger Cook, sheltered by the liberating clause 'in the public interest', has taken the confrontational style of interviewing to unprecedented lengths. Individuals are often secretly filmed and then, with no warning, asked to justify themselves. Fortunately, most of British industry is law-abiding and so is unlikely to become the target of this style of interview.

That doesn't mean, however, that you won't sometimes find yourself in an adversarial situation. For instance, a clash of opinion about the need for a new by-pass potentially creates a lively local radio studio discussion, but it could become confrontational. The skill in dealing with this lies in being sure of your arguments and never allowing yourself verbally to overheat.

➡ INTERVIEW ENVIRONMENTS

As well as understanding different styles of interview, it is useful to know what to expect from the different interview environments, be they live or recorded.

In television these days, live progammming tends to be an exception, which perhaps explains why programme makers go to great lengths to remind the viewer of the novelty by giving incessant verbal time checks. Morning and evening news bulletins and current affairs programmes, Saturday morning children's shows, coverage of state occasions, elections and some sports are live broadcasts; the rest will usually be pre-recorded. Radio, on the other hand, is a medium that lends itself to live broadcasting. The advantage of participating in a live interview is that everything you say will be broadcast and, so long as you are well prepared, a live performance is often sharper than a pre-recorded one. Always check the format for your interview beforehand.

There are advantages and disadvantages to the recorded interview. On the one hand, the studio atmosphere will be less tense and people will be less rushed. The interview can be arranged at a more civilised time of day, which will help you feel less nervous. On the other hand, like a newspaper report or interview, you may have no control over which parts of your contribution will be included or, necessarily, who else might appear in the programme, or at which point during the proceedings you'll be introduced. As will be explained later, there are certain things you can do to try and influence editorial decisions and programme structure.

If you make a factual mistake during a recorded interview, you *must* correct it. Don't be intimidated by mutterings of overtime costs. This is *your* moment and although producers don't like to admit it, they don't want to get it wrong either. It is sometimes as quick and as cost-effective to re-record the whole interview. If this does happen, mentally jettison the first 'take' and clear your mind for the second. The great advantage is that you have the opportunity to either improve on what you've already said, or introduce a new idea. If you can convince the programme producer of either, they will want to re-record.

A live or a recorded media interview can take place in one of a number of venues, each of which is discussed hereafter.

- television studios
- radio studios
- television down the line
- radio down the line
- ISDN lines
- other locations

Television studios

To the inexperienced eye, a television studio is a place designed to look after everyone except you. There is an atmosphere of frenzy and the language is unfamiliar. Snaking black cables, unflinching camera lenses and heat-inducing arc lights all contribute to an atmosphere of fear. The golden rule in a television studio before you go 'on air' is to do as you're told and focus your attention *solely* on your interviewer. Never look into a camera lens unless instructed to, and don't try to engage in humorous banter with the camera crew. Situations that offer no cinematic challenge are anathema to them, so don't expect a reaction; to them, you are simply a 'talking head'.

The most distracting person in the studio is the floor manager. Her job is to relay messages from the director, who literally sits on high in a glass-fronted gallery above the studio floor, to the reporter or presenter. Prior to transmission, the floor manager can talk to everyone; as soon as the red light goes on, she must resort to sign language. The combination of the crouched position below the camera lenses and strange gesticulations make her hard to ignore. It is almost impossible not to take it as a personal criticism when she draws her hand sharply across her throat, as if suggesting decapitation. This gesture is not a judgment of your performance but simply a silent time signal to the presenter that the interview must be brought to an immediate close.

Studio interviewers wear a small ear-piece, through which they receive verbal instructions from the director, and this often accounts for a sudden glazing of the eyes as they try to do two things at once. Don't let their temporary withdrawal of attention unsettle you; simply hold their eye contact and keep talking. You will only need to wear an ear-piece yourself when you do a 'down-the-line' interview.

Television technicians guard their jobs jealously, so when a sound engineer comes to pin a microphone to you, don't attempt to help. TV studio mikes are the same size as those you'd use if you give a presentation using a radio microphone.

People are often concerned about how to sit during a TV interview. Known as the BBC principle (bottom in the back of the chair), the most important thing is to be comfortable and lean *towards* rather than away from the interviewer. Whoever designed the studio couch did not have the guests' interests at heart: it might make the studio set look cosy and informal, but it will do nothing for your appearance as you inevitably slip backwards, sometimes almost to a reclining position. To maintain physical control, sit on the edge of the sofa, both feet on the ground and lean towards the interviewer. Avoidance of the NHG factor (nasty hairy gap) has already been raised.

Just as for a presentation, the clothes you wear for television should suit your own personality and the style of the programme. Don't wear anything that will distract the viewer from what you're saying. Certain colours and patterns are out simply because the camera lens can't cope. Pastel shades always look good, but bold stripes and small checks tend to 'dance' on front of the camera and TV cameras still have difficulty coping with blocks of very bold colours. Black and white next to the face tend to flatten facial features, as well as probably making you look unwell.

Because studios are hot, always try to wear a natural material next to your skin. Nylon creates static, and other artificial fibres tend to cling if you sweat. If you wear glasses, make sure they're clean and, unless you want to be publicly associated with the Mafia, that they aren't the type that darken in bright light. Don't wear clanking jewellery or stuff your top pocket with pens or personal organisers. If your watch is digital, make sure that all bleeping reminders are silenced. And, just as gun-slingers in the Wild West had to part with their accessories before entering the saloon, leave your mobile phone or pager outside. Finally, expect to be made up. Men tend to need it to reduce 'shine' and women to stop their features disappearing.

Radio studios

Radio is a very intimate medium, for listener and participant alike. It is also the least distracting. Not only does the broadcaster give the impression of one-to-one communication, but the listener is considerably allowed to get on with his shaving, tea-making or duvet-turning at the same time. What it lacks, of course, is the colour and movement of television, and the benefits of newspaper photographs and layout. Every picture and emotion has to be created aurally. To help build a sound picture, it is worth remembering a radio cliché that 'when you smile, your voice smiles with you'.

Unlike television (where you are not encouraged to bring notes), it is quite acceptable to use a few index-cards for reference. Don't bring sheaves of paper, as these will rustle and the sound will be picked up by the very sensitive microphones.

It's important that you feel comfortable in your chair and that you can see your interviewer. Radio microphones are intrusive and intimidating, but so long as you don't wander too far from your own, you needn't worry about whether or not you're speaking loudly enough – that's the engineer's job. Eye contact with the interviewer is as important in a radio interview as in a television one. The same rules of focused attention apply: take all your cues from your interviewer and don't be distracted by anyone else.

A final note about dress. Don't assume, just because your audience can't see you, that it doesn't matter what you wear. The way you dress will not only indicate to the interviewer how you feel about yourself and the interview, but it will also affect your performance. Jeans and a sweatshirt suggest informality, a suit means 'business'.

Television down the line

For television and radio companies, down-the-line interviews are a practical and inexpensive way of conducting a conversation. The guest can be in one location and the interviewer in another. The

TV reporter, however, has the unfair advantage of being able to see you in a monitor, whereas you won't be able to see the reporter.

The secret of successful down-the-line interviews is to treat either the radio microphone or the camera as a friend. Doing this adds warmth to your voice and facial expression.

In a TV down-the-line interview, you will be directed to a very small studio, sat in front of a single camera and asked to wear an ear-piece, through which you will hear studio instructions and your interviewer. *You will not be able to see your interviewer.* There is usually a small monitor below your eye-line showing your image. Resist the temptation to look at it, as the action of looking down will make you look shifty. Make sure you are sitting comfortably and then lean very slightly towards the camera. Have the confidence to look directly into the lens. This will give the appearance of talking directly to the viewer. As soon as you can hear the other studio, anything you say could be broadcast, so be circumspect. As down-the-line interviews are often live, there will be little time for preliminary conversation. You may simply hear an instruction '*coming to you in five seconds*', followed by the presenter's introduction and the first question, so be ready.

A down-the-line interview should not be treated as a passport photo-taking session. You are allowed to move your head, gesticulate and smile – anything that will make you look less wooden. And even when you think the interview is over, keep looking in the camera lens for at least five seconds. We've all seen people wrenching out their ear piece and turn anxiously away while the camera is still on them.

I've noticed a growing tendency for people, especially politicians, doing down-the-line interviews to suddenly appear to lose audio contact with the interviewer the moment a tough question comes up. It's not a ploy I would recommend to the inexperienced interviewee!

Radio down the line

The mechanics of a radio interview down the line are the same as for television. Although you can't see your audience, you have to sound as if you can. Find an eye point just above your microphone, and imagine a person in your line of sight whom you like;

then talk to that person rather than to the disembodied voice coming through your headphones. Most BBC down-the-line studios are self-operated, which means that, as well as trying to get your brain together, you have to switch on the equipment. If you are as technically inept as me, the only way to overcome this challenge is to leave plenty of time or, even better, get help.

ISDN lines

ISDN is the acronym for Integrated Services Digital Network. It is an increasingly popular system for carrying information. It can carry many different types of data, including voice, fax and raw computer output. Unlike analogue signal cables, which have to convert digital information to sound before being sent and converted back again at the other end, ISDN lines can transmit digital data 'as is' and permit much higher transmission rates than previously possible.

ISDN delivers sound of broadcast quality, enabling companies to avoid having to send executives to dedicated down-the-line radio studios. By installing ISDN systems in their offices, companies have the opportunity to broadcast directly to radio stations with compatible systems. Costs used to be prohibitive, but it is now possible to install an ISDN system for a few thousand pounds.

Other locations

In theory, a taped conversation conducted on home territory shouldn't cause you as much anxiety as a studio one. However, location TV crews are always in a hurry and seemingly short-staffed. These days, crews consist of a camera operator, a sound person (who often doubles up as a lighting engineer), and a reporter. If the story is part of a documentary, the director or producer might also attend, but on the whole news stories will be covered by a small team.

You will have some control over where the filming takes place. Perhaps the safest location, although visually the least interesting, is your office. You might even be able to position your company logo strategically behind you. If you work in a factory environment and it isn't too noisy, it creates a much more interesting picture to film you next to the production line or in the laboratory. Always make sure that the location adds something to the story. If you are being quizzed on your environmental record, it wouldn't be sensible to do the interview in front of a belching factory chimney; far better that you're seen on the football field of the company sports club.

There are two rules common to both radio and television location interviews: be accommodating, and make sure there are no interruptions.

➡ PRESS INTERVIEWS

Press interviews can be more challenging than radio or television ones for two reasons. They usually last much longer, making room for more mistakes to be made, and they will often be written up as a mixture of straight reporting and observation. As well as preparation, which applies to any interview, there are some simple rules for dealing with print journalists, and these are set out in Checklist 11.1.

Checklist 11.1 Rules for dealing with the press

- Always appear friendly and helpful, especially during the initial enquiry to request a meeting. If possible, try to fix the interview on your territory. Make sure you've familiarised yourself with the publication and, if possible, the journalist's work. Find out if there is a deadline set.

- Anticipate the questions. There are not many types: who, what why, where, when and how. Don't be afraid, when you meet, to find out the journalist's story angle or tell them yours.

- Have in mind three main points and make sure you introduce them and, at the end of the interview, repeat them: 'Is there anything else you need? From my point of view, the three most important areas we've covered are ...'

- Just as with radio and television, treat everything said at the meeting as 'on the record'.

- Don't assume you are the only person the journalist will be talking to.

- Conversely, if you have agreed to give an 'exclusive' interview, keep it that way. Journalists are very sensitive about their 'scoops'.

- Unless there are complicated facts involved, which you have every right to check for accuracy, it is unlikely that a print journalist will send you the copy before it goes to press. The ploy of ringing to find out if she needs any further information sometimes gives you a second bite, but don't rely on it.

- If you're pleased with the outcome, always write and say so.

Telephone interviews with the press tend to be much shorter than face-to-face ones and are beset with traps:

- There is no eye contact.
- You don't know what they are writing down.
- You are pressured into giving an immediate comment.

If a call comes through to you unscreened, you should try to buy some time. Explain that you're not able to talk at that moment, but that you'll ring right back. Find out their name, who they represent and what information they are looking for. Always phone back; failure to do so will inevitably result in a peeved journalist and probably sour copy.

➡ DO YOU WANT TO TALK TO THE MEDIA?

Even though you now have an idea what to expect, you don't *have* to accept every media invitation that comes your way. There may be a legitimate reason why you shouldn't talk. Just as agony aunts in popular magazines advise the 'credit and debit' technique to help the emotionally indecisive, you too should draw up a balance sheet to help you decide, and one is shown in Checklist 11.2. At first sight it's not an easy decision, as both sides of the balance sheet seem equal – except for one vital factor: if you prepare rigorously, the credits will outweigh the debits.

Checklist 11.2   The debit and credit of giving media interviews

Credit	Debit
• It's an opportunity for free publicity.	• It could backfire.
• You have control.	• They will try to take control.
• Editorial coverage adds objective credibility.	• They may not get the message right.
• Talking to the press can put a stop to rumours.	• Talking to the press can inflame rumours.
• You can put the record straight.	• By so doing, you may betray professional confidences.
• You could well be asked back.	• You could fall flat on your face.

There is, of course, no law that says you have to talk. We all know what we think when we hear the oft-repeated phrase, 'We asked Trip-Up & Co. for its opinion, but the firm declined to comment.' However, there are occasions when it will be imprudent to give an interview, such as the pre-posting of annual results, or in relation to sensitive merger discussions or *sub judice* cases, in which case you have to deflect enquiries without incurring either wrath or suspicion from the journalist.

Honesty is often a useful ally in this situation:

I wish I could answer that question personally, but you're talking to the wrong person. You should contact ... .

You can try this ploy, often based on truth:

I would like to talk on your programme, but can you save it for a couple of weeks? As I'm sure you'll appreciate, we're in the middle of stock-taking and up against our own deadlines. If you could ring me back after ... I'd be more than happy to talk to you.

As a final resort, you might try taking the journalist into your confidence and explaining 'off the record' why you're unable at that particular time to help. This is an option that should be exercised *with extreme caution*: if you have built up a relationship of mutual trust with a journalist, it will probably work; if not, think twice before compromising yourself and the journalist.

➡ HOW TO PREPARE FOR A MEDIA INTERVIEW

There are three aspects of preparation, discussed in more detail below:

- Research your audience.
- Prepare your arguments.
- Know your rights.

Research your audience

Researching your audience prior to giving a media interview is as important as finding out about the one that you have been invited to give a presentation to. In the case of an interview, knowing who is going to interview you and who may hear, see or read about you will influence your decision as to whether or not to take part and will enable you to anticipate likely questions. An invitation to appear on BBC 2's *Newsnight* with Jeremy Paxman, for instance, should not automatically be accepted unless you feel confident you can cope with his aggressive style. Being photographed by *Hello!* magazine, on the other hand, would not be a threat.

It is up to you to take the trouble to do your homework. Listen to the programme, video a show or read a journalist's copy. It will be worth the effort.

Prepare your arguments

Until you know what you want to get out of an interview, you will seldom be satisfied by the way you come across. Most of us, because we haven't sorted out our thoughts before talking to someone in the media, fall into the trap of trying to tell the whole story. Not surprisingly, this type of interview usually fails.

Let us suppose that you have been invited to join your local radio breakfast show to talk about the extension to your factory to be opened by your local mayor that afternoon. You've listened to the programme for a couple of days, so you know its style and the presenters' names. You'll know roughly how long each item tends to last and you'll have made sure you know the whereabouts of the radio station. Now write down all the positive things you want to say about the factory extension – you should easily find ten. This will be seven too many, so you must become your own editor. Which three points are the ones you want to make on that radio show or to that local newspaper reporter?

Depending on your audience, the choice of the particular three points will vary. Remember, it mustn't be more than three. Your company's name may be one of them. It's surprising the number of people who give excellent interviews on behalf of their industry, forgetting their own identification, and so bring it in early. This not only relieves you of the burden of trying to remember to introduce the name later, but also gives you the opportunity to link it to something positive. Be careful not to over-promote: broadcasters usually credit you and your company in the introduction to the item and in the back-announcement, and you risk their irritation and subsequent verbal put-down if you are too liberal with the plugs.

The aspect of preparation that most people avoid is the need to address the negative issues. None of us likes admitting that some things are not as they should be but, if you are going to win the media stakes, you *must* face up to them before the interview, not during it. For instance, if you know your interim results are down on last year, be ready to deal with a question challenging your managerial competence. It may not come up, but if it does, at least it won't take you by surprise.

More disconcerting than not being able to deal with a negative question is the terrifying experience of hearing *yourself* introduce one. What follows is something that happened in a recent media training seminar. I was working with three senior hotel executives who had come to learn about dealing with the media and, in particular, about how to deal with a crisis. The first scenario was an outbreak of food poisoning. They were told that 14 of their guests had been rushed to hospital with suspected salmonella poisoning.

Trainee number one was unceremoniously directed into a corridor, where he was greeted by a camera crew and reporter.

Reporter: We've just heard, Mr Jeeves, that 14 of your guests have been rushed to hospital with salmonella poisoning. (*Note the implied statement in the question.*)

Mr Jeeves: (*who begins well*) We don't know that it was salmonella poisoning … .

(*The reporter stares at the interviewee purposefully, willing him to go on, which he obligingly does.*)

Mr Jeeves: Yes, it could perhaps have been an air-borne disease … . (*Mr Jeeves has just dug himself a deep financial hole, into which the reporter is about to let him fall.*)

Mr Jeeves: … Something like Legionnaire's disease … .

We discovered later that Mr Jeeves had unintentionally raised the subject of Legionnaires' disease because it was on his mind and he was anxious about how he would deal with the subject if it *did* come up. The only way to avoid this happening is to take the time not only to isolate negative issues, but to practise answering questions about them.

Know your rights

Over the years, the media have come to accept that, if an interview is to be half-way fair and half-way interesting, then the interviewee must be afforded basic rights. Unfortunately, very few people in the media take the trouble to explain them. This is not because they are being deliberately deceitful, but simply because common courtesies tend to get overlooked in a radio or television studio. These basic rights – and some that do *not* apply – are set out in Checklist 11.3.

Checklist 11.3 **Interviewee rights**

You have a right:

- to know the following:
  - the title and style of the programme on which you've been

asked to appear
- whether the interview is live or recorded
- how long your spot will be
- the broad outline of the interview
- whether it will be a one-to-one or group discussion
- the interviewer's first question
- when the programme will be transmitted;

• to be addressed by the right name;

• to be reported accurately and, if you are not, there are established complaint channels for radio, press and television;

• not to talk to a journalist who gets through to you without prior warning; and

• not to admit a journalist on to private property.

You do not have a right:

• to see a transcript or copy of a programme before it is transmitted;

• to demand a list of questions prior to the interview;

• to insist on not being asked certain questions (you can try, but making a fuss will guarantee they will be asked); or

• to choose at what point you will appear during the programme (unless you are the Prime Minister or Madonna).

---

* Press Complaints Commission, 1 Salisbury Square, London, EC4Y 8AE (tel 0171-353-1248)

Independent Television Commission, 33 Foley Street, London, W1P 7LB (tel 0171-255-3000)

Broadcasting Standards Council and Broadcasting Complaints Commission, 7 The Sanctuary, London, SW1P 3JS (tel 0171-233-0544)

➡ HANDLING AN INTERVIEWER'S TRICKS

From a reporter's perspective, the purpose of an interview is to get as much relevant and lively information as possible. As I have already said, he will probably be working to a predetermined agenda, which will result in a specific line of questioning. If he begins to sense that your answers are not meeting his needs, he will employ various tricks to try to make you say more than you probably should. These are discussed below, but in summary they are:

• the loaded introduction

• changing the first question

- the leading question
- the open question
- the direct question
- the final question
- the pregnant pause

The loaded introduction

Most TV and radio interviewers like the sound of their own voice and an obvious place to show off is when they are introducing an item. A great deal of damage can be done in the 30 seconds it takes to set the scene for your interview – not only because there is no interaction at this point but also because audience attention will be at its height. If a presenter says something in the introduction with which you vehemently disagree, or is factually incorrect, you *must* use your first answer to put the record straight. However, if it's something as trivial as getting your first name wrong, don't waste air-time correcting the mistake.

Changing the first question

In a radio or television interview, as mentioned in Checklist 11.3 it is sometimes possible to find out an interviewer's first question prior to the broadcast or recording. Knowing how she is going to start helps put you at your ease and gives you a chance momentarily to prepare. Very occasionally, you will come up against an unprincipled interviewer who, having told you how she intends to begin, will surprise you by asking something totally different. This is shabby behaviour and, for the inexperienced, can be very unnerving. If it happens and you feel sufficiently aggrieved, let the audience know how you've been misled.

The leading question

Interviewers sometimes find themselves getting carried away on a tide of self-righteous moral campaigning, which finds itself expressed in leading questions:

So, basically your only motivation was profit?

You must be very concerned about the extent of pension mis-selling in your company.

Accusatory questions such as these do *not* have to be answered directly. The important thing is not to repeat the negatives. For example, you shouldn't say: 'Our only motivation is not profit, it is the welfare of our staff. ...' Even though you've denied the allegation, repeating it somehow reinforces it in the audience's mind. Far better to reply, for example,

> Our company mission, for the past decade, has three fundamental elements – loyalty to our staff, innovation and, lastly, profitability. We are proud of those principles ... .'

The open question

The open question tends to be an extended form of the leading question. The interviewer will appear, in a most reasonable manner, to present you with a series of questions that are, in fact, a statement. The skill in dealing with this situation is to be selective. Choose to answer only *one* of the points raised.

> You raised a number of interesting ideas in your question. Let me deal with the one that I found most arresting. ...'

The direct question

Don't be afraid to deflect a direct question. Equally, be prepared to deal with the same question asked differently. If you feel you have genuinely gone as far as you can in your answer, have the confidence politely, but firmly, to tell your interviewer so. Similarly, don't allow yourself to be bullied into divulging sensitive or confidential information. Use a little guile:

Interviewer:	Mr Grossman, just what were your profit margins last year?
Mr Grossman:	I don't think my accountants would be too happy if I divulged that information. What I am able to tell you is that turnover is up and we've added twenty more people to our wage bill.

The final question

Most journalists will let you know when an interview is coming to an end, and mean it. Sometimes, however, for reasons beyond their control they will continue to ask questions even though they have signalled that the conversation is about to end.

For instance: 'One final question, when do you see your company going on the AIM?' You answer the question to the best of your ability and begin to wind down, only to be brought abruptly to attention with another qustion: 'So you streamlined your work force to make the prospectus look more attractive. How many people did you make redundant?' It is certainly a surprise and it might be below the belt, but you shouldn't have assumed the interview was over, or let your concentration lapse, until the presenter moved to the next item.

The pregnant pause

The pregnant pause is a simple but effective way of provoking an interviewee to say more than intended. The reporter asks a question, listens to the answer and then, saying nothing, looks directly at the subject, letting the answer hang in the air. This silence makes the interviewee feel awkward, so as to rush in and fill the silence, often with unfortunate consequences.

It is just as much the reporter's responsibility as it is yours to keep an interview going. If you have made a point, have the confidence to look him in the eye, stay quiet, and wait for the next question. It will come.

➡ TECHNIQUES FOR ANSWERING QUESTIONS

Answering questions in a media interview should be treated in the same way as speaking in public; the preparatory process is also similar. You have researched your audience and the programme, worked out what you want to say, and practised. The only difference is that you have to get your message across via an intermediary. So long as they are prepared, most people find this type of public communication far less taxing than giving a solo presentation. This is probably because, although it is artificial, an interview *feels* more natural.

How you answer the questions is, of course, very important. Politicians, as I have indicated, often only pay lip service to the protocol of interviews and therefore seldom answer a question. It is essential that you always are seen to attempt to answer each question. You shouldn't have any difficulty with straightforward questions. 'Why are you expanding in the North East?' can be easily answered. On the other hand, 'Why are you expanding in the North East when, only last week, your regional director told a local reporter that there were no prospects ... ?' is much more problematical.

There is a technique for answering difficult questions, for questions to which you don't know the answer, for moving the interview along or for bringing in one of your three points. It is known as the 'AA technique', standing for Acknowledgement and Action. It must be used sparingly, or the reporter will smell a media-trained rat.

Although much shorter, the 'acknowledgement' is as important as the 'action'. It is the 'acknowledgement' that signals to the interviewer that you have registered the question. The 'action' is where you take control. Here are some examples of the AA technique.

> You're quite right, it has been a problem (*acknowledgement*) but, as our recent figures show, we now lead the field. Indeed, with our acquisition of the plant in Bangkok, the future looks even brighter (*action*).

> That's an interesting question but, first, can I put it into perspective? ... (*acknowledgement/action*).

> I'm glad you asked me that, because it brings me to a point I've been wanting to make ... (*acknowledgement/action*).

> I really think I've done my utmost to deal with that point. There is nothing more I can tell you about it at the moment. What I *am* able to talk about is ... .' (*acknowledgement/action*).

Of course, these bridging phrases will only help if you know what you want to say. If you do, they will buy you precious thinking time to recall one of your key messages, and enable you to get out of a potentially difficult situation.

As well as believing that you can control your answers, you should consider:

- content and length
- avoiding negative triggers
- truth
- the last word

Content and length

A question must never be answered with a bald 'yes' or 'no'. If a journalist asks a question that can elicit such a conversation-stopper, she is not doing her job.

Answers must never contain more than one point. It amuses me when I hear someone limbering up for a three-point reply, as I know he won't get as far as the third. In all interviews, no answer should be longer than 60 seconds, preferably 30. There is always a temptation to be expansive with the press, and it is true that the environment lends itself to a more conversational style than radio or television, but never lose sight of the main purpose of the interview, to get *your* messages across. If you confuse the journalist with too much detail, you may not succeed in your aim.

Although you have less time, illustrations, anecdotes and striking statistics are just as important in an interview as they are in a presentation. So is the language you use: no jargon, sparing use of the royal 'we', and awareness of irritating personal verbal habits such as 'I mean/you know/at the end of the day'.

Avoiding negative triggers

There are certain words and phrases that should be avoided, because they ring automatic warning bells in a perceptive interviewer's ear. These are

- disappointing
- satisfactory
- unexpected
- unconfirmed
- hopefully
- reasonable
- uncertain
- unresolved

Truth

If you don't know something, don't make it up. Say something like, 'I'm sorry, I don't have that information on me, but if you'd like to phone my office in the morning, I can certainly try to help ... .' And don't lie. You may not be caught out the first, second or even third time, but once you are, it will be a long, hard haul back to credibility.

The last word

Some unprincipled presenters will try to turn the knife at the end of an interview, in the mistaken belief that you won't have the temerity to challenge them. If, in your opinion, a presenter does try to close the interview with a snide, unfair remark, you *must* respond, even though you've been led to believe the programme is over. There is always time for a five-second 'Now, you *know* that's not the case.'

Remember, it's the last image that the viewer or listener takes away from the programme item, and so it is important to make sure it is in your favour.

➡ THE PARTY'S OVER

Appearing on radio or television, or being interviewed by the press, can be a traumatic experience, provoking unguarded exclamations at the end. Maintain your composure until you are sure that the interview is over by looking at the presenter. This will feel unnatural, but it will stop you doing something that might make you look silly.

➡ WHAT NEXT?

Being interviewed by the media is potentially as rewarding as making a presentation, so long as:

- you prepare
- you research your audience
- you decide on a maximum of three key messages
- you identify and deal with the negatives before the interview
- you assert your rights
- you believe you can be in control.

The occasion when you need both media and presentation skills is at a press conference or press briefing. Techniques for handling either situation are discussed in the next chapter.

Chapter 12
How to Hold a Press Conference or Press Briefing

Imparting information to a group rather than individually obviously saves time and money. A gathering also creates a sense of occasion, which is the right atmosphere for a press conference.

You might consider holding one in the following circumstances.

- to launch a product, book, fund, prize, charity or political campaign;
- to disclose company news – a merger, a management buy-out, job creation;
- to keep the media informed about a crisis;
- to clear the air, explain a controversy, scotch a rumour; and
- to reveal the scoop of the century – a newly-discovered play by Shakespeare, the real site of Camelot, Lord Lucan's whereabouts, etc.

There is no point holding one unless you have good reason in comparison with other forms of information transfer. Some of the valid reasons are given in Checklist 12.1.

Checklist 12.1 **Reasons for holding a press conference**
- You have something to announce that can't be adequately covered in a press release.
- The news warrants a press conference rather than a press briefing.

- You have something to say that will benefit from detailed elaboration.
- You have anticipated and are able to deal confidently with questions.
- You choose the timing and venue with care.

➡ SETTING UP A PRESS CONFERENCE

Once you have decided that you have something to announce that is best dealt with by a press conference, you need to consider various elements of setting one up properly. These are:

- When to hold the conference.
- Where to hold the conference.
- How to select spokespeople.
- Incentives to attend.
- The invitation.
- Arrangements on arrival and departure.

The practical implications of each of these elements are discussed below, before I turn to the formal presentation and the question-and-answer session that normally follows.

When to hold the conference

However carefully you plan the timing of a press conference, there is no guarantee that your story won't be eclipsed by something more newsworthy. To limit this uncertainty, avoid days of public importance, such as Budget day, polling days or public holidays.

If you want to make the evening papers, your deadline is about noon. TV news desks need at least two hours to edit material ready for transmission. So a morning conference, to take advantage of the one o'clock bulletins, should start no later than 10 a.m. Be aware of these TV deadlines and try and give crews the first interviews after the formal presentations.

Where to hold the conference

Use a little intelligence when choosing the venue for the press conference. Try and make it as accessible as possible for media representatives, and be sure that it is well-equipped with phones, faxes, ISDN lines, and good audio-visual facilities. The size of the room is also important: if it is too large, it will be difficult to fill, giving the impression of lack of interest; if it is too small, everyone will feel uncomfortable.

Make sure that the platform height is to your liking and that the lectern and autocue screens are adjustable. Great care should be taken over the seating arrangements. As a rule, speakers should be seated at a top table, on a slightly raised platform facing the audience. Their identification cards must be written in letters large enough to be read from the back of the room. The lectern and visual aid equipment should be set up close to the top table so that speakers can easily hand over to each other. A press conference audience is usually seated cinema-style.

How to select spokespeople

There are some occasions, such as a crisis update or reporting on a patient's medical condition, where only one spokesperson is necessary. In less urgent situations, it is sensible to have more. One main speaker, supported by one or two colleagues works well.

Always find the right spokespeople. Hierarchies are part of business life, but if your company's Chairman is an ineffectual speaker, make sure that the main presentations and interviews are given to other members of the team.

Incentives to attend

On 25 January 1961, J.F. Kennedy became the first US President to allow his press conferences to be televised. Attendance figures rocketed, not least because it gave the journalists the opportunity to become stars as well.

Today incentives are the promise of a newsworthy story, accessible location, interviewees, and photo opportunities. Even the lure of lavish refreshment isn't really necessary any more, although everyone will appreciate being looked after.

The invitation

Journalists get a lot of invitations and are not good at replying to them, which makes estimating numbers difficult. On average, you can expect about one-third of those you invite to turn up.

Take care over the wording and design of the invitation. An impersonal note to the 'Features Editor' is less likely to get a response than a personalised one. Hand-write the guest's name rather than print it. Keep the details clear and to the point: journalists want to know why they have been invited, where they should go, and what time they should arrive. Include a map and contact number. If a press release is likely to spoil the element of surprise, enclose a descriptive 'teaser' instead.

Always keep a copy of the invitation list, not only to chase those who haven't replied, but for future reference.

Arrangements on arrival and departure

Even though the formal proceedings won't have begun, first impressions will have been made the moment journalists walk into the room. Be sure there is someone to greet them and show them to their seats. Ask them to sign the visitors' book and give them a name badge. Colour coding is sensible (e.g. green for the press, red for staff and blue for dignitaries).

If there are TV or radio journalists present, find out their deadlines and try to accommodate them. Even though you hope ITN may turn up, you should start the first part of the conference not later than ten minutes after the stated time, and finish on time.

It is hospitable to offer refreshments. Depending on the time of day, coffee on the way in is always appreciated and a light snack and alcoholic drink on the way out. It is essential that all company spokespeople stay for this session, not only to network but to answer journalists' individual questions. However tempting, remember the rule about no alcohol for the company representatives.

If you're providing hospitality in another room, make sure there are enough seats and also quiet corners where individual interviews can be conducted. Although post-press conference gatherings tend to be less stressful than the formal presentation, never forget that it is still a public function and that anything you say is 'on the record'. This is the time when journalists will want to pursue their individual angles. Be as helpful as you can, but remember that your rights still apply. If there is something you can't answer, then don't attempt to do so. Either divert them or promise to ring later.

Press packs and product samples should be given as the journalists leave. Always include copies of the presentations, product samples and a contact number.

➡ THE FORMAL PRESENTATION

Presenting to a group of journalists shouldn't, in theory, be different from addressing any other group. But it is. Journalists have a vested interest in attending a press conference. They are looking for information that will be of interest to their viewers, listeners or readers. They are therefore likely to be more attentive and more critical than other audiences. They will also have already begun to think about their angle for the story and will be alert to anything you say that will corroborate it.

Remember that they will all have different deadlines and different levels of knowledge and expertise. General news reporters may cover more than one story in a day, and so they will always be in a hurry. To pitch your presentation at the right level, go back to the basic structural rules already covered in Chapter 4:

- greeting (──)
- menu (●)
- housekeeping (▲)
- body of speech (▬)
- summary (■)
- conclusion (✚)

Keep your language simple and colourful. You need to *perform* as much for a media audience as you do a general one. On the whole, journalists have a somewhat jaundiced view of life, believing that they really have already 'done it, seen it and got the T-shirt', and so it is very important to make an impact.

➡ THE QUESTION-AND-ANSWER SESSION

The question-and-answer session in a press conference is as important as the formal presentation, and you must anticipate and rehearse both the questions and the answers. Decide who will be in the chair and who will deal with specific subjects. There is nothing more frustrating than watching a panel trying to decide who will answer a question. Always make a note of a questioner's name and which publication or programme they represent. If the hall requires a roving microphone, make sure there is one and someone to operate it.

It is very important in your 'housekeeping' notes to remind the journalists how long the session will last and what back-up information they can expect. The chairperson must control the questions. For instance, if you are only going to allow one question per speaker, let the audience know beforehand. Remind speakers not to ask a question until the roving microphone has reached them, and insist on them giving their name and who they represent.

Hosts of press conferences are always fearful that people either won't turn up or, if they do, won't ask any questions. The most common reasons for an initial lack of questions are either the fear that the enquiry will expose lack of concentration or because a journalist doesn't want to reveal the angle of his story. The rhetorical question is a good ploy to get things going. Alternatively, have a couple of 'plants', colleagues in the audience ready with one or two. Once the ice is broken, there will always be questions.

If you are in the chair, it is very important to lead from the front. You must let your audience know which questioner you will be going to next, how much time has elapsed and how many questions may still be asked. If someone is trying to monopolise the time available, politely but firmly move on to someone else. If a question is either inaudible or unintelligible, don't hesitate to repeat it in your own words.

Each spokesperson has a responsibility to listen attentively during the question-and-answer session. It is all too easy, while a colleague is performing, to 'switch off' and start planning next year's holiday. Lack of concentration usually manifests itself as either extreme boredom or deep depression. Don't underestimate how difficult it is to look interested. Natural inhibition will tend to suppress silent gestures of encouragement, but you must not allow it to do so. However unnatural it may feel, do make a concerted effort to look at the speaker, nod in agreement, smile at his humorous remarks (even though you heard them last week), and appear to make the occasional note. An attentive panel helps both the speaker and his audience.

As the time for questions draws to a close, use the final moments to recap on the key elements of the conference. You may be fortunate and be talking to a group of journalists who are grateful not to have to go back through their notes, or whose memories will be effectively jogged by the recap.

➡ THE PRESS BRIEFING

Press briefings tend to be smaller and less formal occasions than press conferences, although the objectives are the same: to make the media aware of either your product or your organisation. Although the briefing session will be informal, don't underestimate the importance of planning. And like a press conference, whatever you say will always be 'on the record'.

The most successful press briefings usually involve four to five journalists and take place over a meal or drink. To avoid the competitive element, don't ask four features editors from four national newspapers. Far better to vary the mix by bringing together someone from a daily paper, and others from a monthly magazine, a trade publication and a local paper. This will enable each journalist to pursue his own angle.

➡ THE END RESULTS

If you've followed the advice in this chapter, picking up the papers the morning after your press conference could come as a pleasant surprise. If you're accurately and fairly reported, take the trouble to write and say thank you. Who knows, you could soon find yourself on *Newsnight*!

Appendix A
Twenty golden rules
for effective presentations

1. Find out as much as you can about the audience and other speakers.
2. Establish the precise location of the venue and availability of audio-visual facilities.
3. Get a clear brief from your host.
4. Think before you write.
5. Structure your speech before starting to write: greeting/ menu/housekeeping/main points/summary/conclusion.
6. Write as you speak.
7. Time your first draft; revise the text according to the time available.
8. Keep visual aids simple and remember they are to benefit your audience, not you.
9. Anticipate questions.
10. Try out your speech on an honest friend.
11. Rehearse.
12. Develop a personal relaxation routine.
13. Wear something you know you look good in.
14. Allow plenty of time to get to the venue.
15. Check that all equipment is working before you begin.
16. Don't eat fast foods or drink alcohol beforehand.
17. Take a spare copy of your presentation.
18. Smile as you walk on stage.
19. Maintain eye contact with your audience.
20. Perform as if your life depended on it.

Appendix B
Selected correct verbal forms of address

The following are taken from *Debrett's New Guide to Etiquette and Modern Manners*, by John Morgan (Headline, UK, 1996)

Her Majesty The Queen **Your Majesty**
His Royal Highness The Prince of Wales **Your Royal Highness**
Lord (& Lady) Mayor **My Lord Mayor**
Lady Mayoress (i.e. Wife of Mayor) **Lady Mayoress**
Police Commissioner **Commissioner/Sir Henry**
Commander, Chief Superintendent **Chief Superintendent/Mr *Tunic***
Chief Inspector **Chief Inspector/Mrs *Truncheon***
The Pope **Your Excellency**
Cardinal **Your Eminence**
Archbishop **Your Grace/Archbishop**
Bishop **My Lord/Bishop *Purple***
The Chief Rabbi **Chief Rabbi**
Rabbi **Rabbi *Rubenstein*/Dr *Rubenstein***
Admiral **Sir *David*/Admiral *Destroyer* (if not a knight)**
The Prime Minister **Prime Minister**
The Chancellor of the Exchequer **Chancellor**
Member of Parliament **Mr *Party-Hack***
The Lord Chancellor **Lord Chancellor**
The Lord Chief Justice of England **Lord Chief Justice**
High Court Judge **Mr *Scribe***
Circuit Judge **Judge**
Queen's Counsel **Mr *Oath***
Marquess **Lord *Malaprop***
Marchioness **Lady *Malaprop***
Life Peer **Lord *Widget***

Appendix C
Sample speech

What follows is a 'template' for a 20-minute presentation using computer-generated graphics to a business audience. Its structure, however, could be adapted to suit most types of presentation. For instance, if you were writing an after-dinner speech, you wouldn't need to deal with 'housekeeping' (▲) and your main points (■■) would probably be anecdotal rather than instructional, but you would, of course, need a strong greeting (—) and conclusion (✦).

The presentation is set out in camera-script style, with the text on the right-hand side of the page and subheadings and personal and visual-aid cues on the left. The text is in 1½-line spacing to allow information to be absorbed by you quickly and relayed to an audience without appearing to read it. The six sections of the speech are marked with their symbols for the same reason.

Although the setting is fictional, the background information below is the kind needed before planning such a presentation.

Peter Pokiss is International Business Director of Global Imprint Corporation (GIC Inc). The company began its life in regional newspapers and has since acquired two national titles and a cable TV channel. Its latest acquisition is an advertising agency. Part of Peter Pokiss' responsibility is 'new business', and his focus for this particular presentation is on generating new business for the advertising agency.

He has embarked on a world trip visiting regional offices, spending two days at each one and talking to groups of 20–30 people. His main presentation is at 9 a.m. on the first day of each visit and he talks for about 20 minutes with the aid of simple, fast-moving computer-generated graphics.

He has a personality profile of each agency and knows its standing in the advertising agency league table. He is aware that many members of staff are suspicious of him, so is absolutely clear that the object of his presentation is to motivate, not criticise.

The essence of the speech he might give follows below. Not all of its content is included for brevity's sake, nor are the slides he would use shown. But the way in which his speech has been constructed in its six elements (with their symbols – see p 49 for key), and a flavour of how he might get some of his points across, have been included. These aspects are reflected in the notes for his speech that follow:

GREETING	SMILE	SLIDE 1.	
—			Good morning everyone. Good to meet you at last.
			Welcome to 'NEW BUSINESS – OUR LIFE BLOOD', the title of my presentation.
			As Richard just said, my name is PETER POKISS, and I'm worldwide business Director for Global Imprint Corporation – GIC. Put that another way. I'm PETER POKISS, and it's **my** job that's on the line if I don't manage to persuade everyone of the importance of new business to GIC, and GIC ADVERTISING in particular.
	PAUSE		
ANECDOTE			The other day, someone asked me if I had any golden rules about winning new business.
			'I have many' I said, 'the most important one being that I *think* first, and *act* later.'

MENU ●	PAUSE
	PAUSE
HOUSE KEEPING ▲	PAUSE
1st MAIN POINT ■ **NEW BUSINESS CENTRAL TO FUTURE**	PAUSE LOOK AROUND AUDIENCE

...

In the next 20 minutes or so, I will address all those valuable comments and also look at **three key areas** that I believe will determine how we approach new business in the future.

Firstly, I'll expand on why I believe we have to make new business central to our future business strategy.

Secondly, I'll demonstrate how well positioned we are already to take up the challenge, and ...

Thirdly, I'll outline what we'll be doing in the future to make sure that we have the infrastructure to make it all happen.

This is an informal discussion – so feel free to ask any questions as we go along.

So, why do I believe so passionately that new business is *central to our* future business strategy?

Over the past months, Richard Bowles has set us three objectives:

		SLIDE 6	**To be among the top five creatively in every market where we operate.**
		SLIDE 7	**To be the best international network.**
		SLIDE 8	**To develop a culture of teamwork and commitment to excellence.**

...

Maybe if I explain my daily commitment to generating new business, it'll be clearer. **I try and nurture at least three key contacts a day.** They might be prospective clients, major market influencers, or I may just want to say 'hello'.

You might find it difficult at first but, once it becomes a habit, you'll soon reap the benefits.

PAUSE

BRIDGE

That's all very well, you are probably thinking, but how can we be proactive when we don't know what kind of agency we really want to be?

2nd
MAIN
POINT
▬

You're right to ask that question. None of us can seek out new business with confidence unless we all know what this agency really stands for.

| | PAUSE | | ... |

What is missing?

I'll tell you. If we were to rely solely on what we have today to win new accounts, we would soon find ourselves struggling.

3rd
MAIN
POINT
▬

Which brings me to the final part of this presentation – the **'bottom line'** if you like.

RESOURCES
(highlight)

What is this agency going to do for you to help you meet Richard's new business challenge?

I drew up a list especially for this meeting, and its extent almost surprised, even me.

New Business Directors: as you probably know, we have pledged to appoint New Business Directors in all our offices by the end of the year. Once on board, they will have an opportunity to attend an intensive three-day 'brain-storming' seminar.

Think tank: as well as appointing New Business Directors, ten of our Managing Directors have joined together as a Think Tank, committed to making sure there is a viable international marketing strategy that can be applied locally.

Intranet: I'm delighted to be able to report that, by the end of the year 'office will be able to speak unto office' via our intranet. (Just as an aside, intranet is not as yet a word that is accepted by the computer – it will have to soon). This will mean that we can each benefit from each other's experiences and tap into each other's client base. This way we can ensure a consistent approach to our marketing – which will mean less duplication; less waste of resources and? ... ... You've got it, **more business.**

PAUSE

MAIN
SUMMARY
■

From the time I joined GIC as New Business Director, I have been able to identify its unique qualities. I am clear what we already have in place to begin to make a much more serious commitment to generate new business than we have ever done before.

I am absolutely **determined** to fight, not only for myself, but for everyone else in this room this morning, for support – both technical and intellectual – to make sure we can achieve Richard's

	EMPHASIZE	SLIDE 20	
	PAUSE		
CONCLUSION ✚			

goals, which, in the unlikely event that you'd forgotten what they are:

• **To make GIC ADVERTISING the best known brand on the block.**
• **To develop – through team work – a consistently high standard of innovation and creativity.**
• **To become a world leader** in communications.

Thank you for giving me the opportunity to share my thoughts with you about why we must take the new business challenge so seriously.

If you succeed, then so do I – and vice-versa. So, let's go to it.

Thank you – and now for questions.

Index